BOLOGNA
POCKET GUIDE

Walking Eye
mobile app

Discover the world's best destinations with the Insight Guides Walking Eye app, available to download for free in the App Store and Google Play.

The container app provides easy access to fantastic free content on events and activities taking place in your current location or chosen destination, with the possibility of booking, as well as the regularly-updated Insight Guides travel blog: Inspire Me. In addition, you can purchase curated, premium destination guides through the app, which feature local highlights, hotel, bar, restaurant and shopping listings, an A to Z of practical information and more. Or purchase and download Insight Guides eBooks straight to your device.

TOP 10 ATTRACTIONS

SANTO STEFANO
Enchanting complex of medieval churches, cloisters and crypts. See page 47.

LE DUE TORRI
The Two Towers are celebrated symbols of the city. Climb to the top of Torre degli Asinelli for splendid views. See page 42.

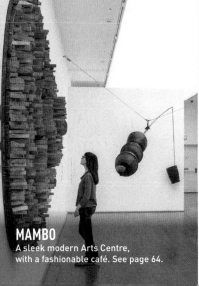

MAMBO
A sleek modern Arts Centre, with a fashionable café. See page 64.

THE PORTICI
An impressive 35km (22 miles) of elegant porticoes provide handy protection from the elements. See page 37.

GASTRONOMY
Indulge in Bologna's culinary delights and find out why they call the city 'La Grassa' (The Fat). See pages 91 and 100.

NEPTUNE'S FOUNTAIN
Giambologna's bronze of Neptune is a favourite rendezvous in the heart of the city. See page 29.

SAN LUCA
Climb the world's longest portico to the hilltop sanctuary church of San Luca. See page 72.

PALAZZO DELL'ARCHIGINNASIO
Former university building with an Anatomical Theatre where human corpses were dissected. See page 38.

BASILICA DI SAN PETRONIO
The monumental basilica ranks among the most imposing of Italy's Gothic churches. See page 34.

PINACOTECA NAZIONALE
The city's finest art collection with works by Bolognese and other Italian masters. See page 56.

A PERFECT DAY

9am

Noon

Breakfast

Kick off the day with coffee and diet-busting brioches at the Caffè Sette Chiese on Piazza Santo Stefano. Secure a seat under the arches of the portico for fine views of Santo Stefano church.

Culinary delights

Plunge into the maze of medieval alleys off Piazza Maggiore with tantalising delis, fresh food stalls and a chic covered food hall. For lunch grab a *piadina* (sandwich) crammed with Parma Ham, Mortadella and local cheeses, or head for Tamburini at Via Caprarie 1, a famous gourmet deli and café.

10am

11am

2pm

Strada Maggiore

From Via Santo Stefano take the Corte Isolani, a medieval warren of galleries and cafés, to Strada Maggiore, lined with porticoes and palazzi. Browse in elegant antique shops and/or visit the delightful Museum of Music and Gothic Church of Santa Maria della Vita.

Historic core

Head for Piazza del Nettuno, host to Giambologna's celebrated statue of Neptune, and beyond to Piazza Maggiore, which is overlooked by the Basilica di San Petronio. Here, absorb everyday life in the square, then take a peek inside the monumental interior of San Petronio.

Ancient university

Take elegant Via dell' Archiginnasio and visit the frescoed Palazzo dell' Archiginnasio, first seat of Bologna's university and where, in the Teatro Anatomico, some of the earliest dissections in Europe were performed. Have coffee and cake at Zanarini, an upmarket café on Piazza Galvani.

University quarter

4pm

Wander along Via Zamboni for a flavour of the university. Pass noble palaces converted to bustling faculties, bohemian bars, eclectic cafés and arty bookshops.

Aperitivo time

6pm

Head to Le Stanze, the private chapel of the Palazzo Bentivoglio at Via del Borgo di San Pietro 1, for a unique combination of cocktails and 16th-century frescoes.

Jazz in the cellar

10pm

Listen to the best live jazz in Bologna at Cantina Bentivoglio, Via Mascarella 4/B, in the antique cellars of the Palazzo Bentivoglio.

Leaning towers

3pm

Head northeast to the Due Torri and gawp at the tipsy towers. Offload a few calories by taking the 480 steps to the top of Torre degli Asinelli. Wander around the nearby former Jewish Ghetto, now home to some delightful artisan workshops.

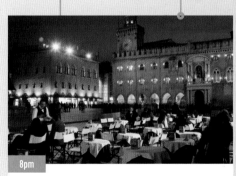

Trusty trattoria

8pm

Close by, dine on fabulous Bolognese pasta (made on the spot as you will see) at Dal Biassanot, Via Piella. Beside the restaurant take a peek through the Finestrella (little window) di Via Piella over the canal and you might believe you were in Venice.

CONTENTS

▥ **Introduction** 10

▥ **A Brief History** 17

▥ **Where to Go** 29
   ❶ *Numbered map references pinpoint the sights*

Piazza Maggiore and Around 29
Piazza del Nettuno 29, Palazzo di Re Enzo and Palazzo del Podestà 30, Palazzo d'Accursio 31, Salaborsa 33, Piazza Maggiore 34, Basilica di San Petronio 34, Museo Civico Archeologico 36, Palazzo dell'Archiginnasio 38, Quadrilatero 39, Santa Maria della Vita 41

East of Piazza Maggiore 41
Due Torri 42, Piazza della Mercanzia 44, Strada Maggiore 44, Museo Internazionale e Biblioteca della Musica 45, Museo Civico d'Arte Industriale e Galleria Davia Bargellini 46, Santa Maria dei Servi 46, Santo Stefano 47

The University Quarter 50
San Giacomo Maggiore 51, Oratorio di Santa Cecilia 52, Piazza Verdi and Teatro Comunale 53, Palazzo Poggi 54, Pinacoteca Nazionale 56

North and West of Centre 59
The Jewish Ghetto 59, Cattedrale Metropolitana di San Pietro 60, Palazzo Fava 61, Museo Civico Medievale 62, San Colombano 63, MAMbo 64, San Francesco 66

South of the Centre 66
Basilica San Domenico 69, Via d'Azeglio 71

The Bologna Hills 72

Excursions from Bologna 73
Parma 74, Modena 76, Ferrari Museums 78, Ferrara 79, Ravenna 83, Rimini 85

What to Do 87

Entertainment 87

Shopping 90

Sport 95

Children's Bologna 98

Eating Out 100

A–Z Travel Tips 115

Recommended Hotels 136

Index 143

Features

A Medieval Manhattan 15
Bologna 'La Dotta' ('The Learned') 21
Historical Landmarks 27
City of Porticoes 37
Where Time Stands Still 40
Mozart and Martini 45
Marconi: Bologna's Wireless Pioneer 55
Bologna and the Baroque 58
A Subterranean Serenissima 63
Genus Bononiae, Museums in the City 68
Aperitivo Time 90
Pasta Perfect 93
Calendar of Events 99
Parma – Haven of Gastronomy 100
Far From Baloney 103

INTRODUCTION

Capital of Emilia Romagna, arguably the most civilised region of Italy, Bologna is renowned for its university, its cuisine and its traditional left-wing stance. Hence the oft-quoted sobriquets: Bologna 'La Dotta' (the Learned), Bologna 'La Grassa' (the Fat), and Bologna 'La Rossa' (the Red). The city is also famous for its beautifully preserved historic centre, and La Rossa refers as much to the rich red of its palaces, towers and porticoes as it does to its left-leaning politics.

Located on the edge of the Po Plain at the foot of the Apennines, the city is a fine example of Roman and medieval town planning, with its ancient town gates, radial plan and long straight streets. It stands on the Via Emilia, the arrow-straight road laid down by the Romans from Rimini to Piacenza. In the Middle Ages this was where Europe's first university was established, and a town quickly grew around it. Dozens of towers rose above the city, built both as watchtowers and as status symbols by the succession of dynasties that ruled Bologna until it became part of the papal states in 1506. The city prospered from its setting, surrounded by fertile plains and vineyards which supplied its convivial inns. Within its walls, urban life was more liberal than in most other provincial cities and a free-thinking entrepreneurial people flourished. Today Bologna is a progressive modern city with a vibrant student population, thriving professional and business sectors and a buzzing street life.

BOLOGNA LA GRASSA

Of the three sobriquets Bologna is perhaps best known globally as 'La Grassa', a reference to its rich culinary tradition. Prosperous Emilia Romagna is the legendary bread basket of Italy, a region which has given birth to culinary delights such as *prosciutto crudo* (Parma ham), Parmesan cheese and world-renowned balsamic vinegar. Emilian cuisine reaches its height in Bologna which is widely acclaimed as the culinary capital of Italy. It is famed for fragrant pink Mortadella, *ragù* (the real Bolognese meat sauce) but above all else for egg pasta. *Tortellini* alone would be a good enough reason to visit Bologna. Legends abound as to the pasta's origins, one of which gives credit to a young cook of a wealthy Bolognese merchant who modelled the pasta on the perfect navel of his master's wife – which even if apocryphal, says much about the seductiveness of the cuisine. *Sfogline* (pasta ladies) in trattorias or pasta shops can still be seen rolling out sheets of pasta and cutting out the tiny delicate shapes. Flourishing pasta cookery schools (there are 25 in the city) and the annual pasta-making competition, *Il Matterello d'Oro* (The Golden Rolling Pin), are further evidence that the home-made *tortellini* is in good shape.

The view over to Piazza Maggiore from the Asinelli tower

A stroll through the teeming medieval streets of the central Mercato di Mezzo reveals tantalising food stores and market stalls brimming with gleaming fresh produce. Gourmet delis are crammed with whole hanging hams and great wheels of cheese, enticing passers-by to stop for a few slices of wafer-thin *prosciutto*, washed down perhaps with a cool glass of Pignoletto. When it comes to restaurants it's not so much about Michelin-rosetted temples of cuisine with exotic new delicacies but earthy family-run trattorias, where the cuisine is simple and the emphasis is on perfect ingredients. While a handful of places in the city give a nod to lighter contemporary cuisine, Bologna for the most part carries on serving what it's best at, and at a leisurely pace.

CULTURAL LEGACY

The city is as passionate about culture as it is about food and enjoys a long tradition of intellectual enlightenment. The medieval lawyers, scholars and sculptors of its university paved the way for scientific breakthroughs that helped shape the modern world and it was the university that was the city's economic powerhouse. The elaborately sculpted sarcophagi of great scholars in the city's Medieval Museum give some idea of the importance attached to academia. Professors rose through the social ranks and were richly rewarded in death as well as life.

The medieval era also witnessed the rise of fine monuments, great Gothic churches rich in art and the characteristic colonnades. These elegant porticoes, now a Unesco

Perfect pasta

The Bolognesi take their food very seriously. In 1972 the Accademia Italiana della Cucina (Academy of Italian Cuisine) decreed that the exact width of a cooked strand of *tagliatelle* must be 1/1,270th of the height of the Asinelli tower, 9mm (0.3 in).

World Heritage Site, have always provided a refuge from the elements and a meeting place for Bolognesi from all backgrounds. In times gone by they provided cover for furtive assassinations and the amorous assignments, of among others, Boccaccio and the Marquis de Sade. Here Verdi and Rossini trampled the porticoed streets in search of inspiration, just as the late novelist Umberto Eco set out in search of material for his medieval whodunits. In the summer months musicians strike up under the arcades, artists set up easels,

Neptune's Fountain

and all year round there is a lively café scene with tables spilling out under the porticoes, assured of shelter from rain, snow or the intense heat of the summer sun.

Thanks to the porticoes and the compact size of the historic centre, Bologna is a delightful city for strolling. There are sufficient monuments, museums and artistic treasures for several days' exploration. Many of the city's churches are rich repositories of art while Renaissance or baroque palazzi, often embellished with frescoes, make fine settings for the city's main museums. Palazzo Poggi, seat of the university, is home to some fascinating specialist museums while the nearby Pinacoteca houses the city's finest art collection, with works by Giotto, Raphael and the great Bolognese painters. In the Baroque period the artistic output flourished here and Bologna

Colourful fresh produce

became the pre-eminent influence in Italian painting.

A LIVING CITY

Despite its illustrious history, wealth of architecture and gastronomic reputation Bologna attracts far fewer tourists than cities such as Florence or Venice. As a result it feels far more Italian, gritty and real and less museum-like, making an enticing alternative to these more famous cities. Fears of arid scholarship are banished by the buzz of the student area, with bohemian bars overlooking faculties tucked into frescoed palaces. Bolognesi of all ages come out for the evening *passeggiata*, the ritual stroll; there's a vibrant café and bar scene, an action-packed calendar of events with concerts, jazz, theatre and art exhibitions and a lively gay scene. In term time the population of 376,000 (1 million in greater Bologna) swells by around 100,000. But even during holiday time there's plenty going on and the Bè Bolognaestate festival from June to September ensures a summer of music, art and theatre. The city has a rich music heritage and has played host to the likes of Verdi, Rossini and Puccini. In 2006 it was appointed Unesco Creative City of Music, a prestigious recognition that honours the city's music tradition – as well as the lively contemporary scene.

Created on the back of agricultural wealth the regional economy has thrived for centuries but always moved with the times. Engineering is a regional strength but embraces everything from cutting-edge car manufacture to machine tools and precision robotics. Emilia Romagna is serious car country, with Ferrari, Maserati and Lamborghini all produced here. The city and the region have always been committed to making both money and desirable products, from Mortadella cured meat to Ducati motorbikes, while not neglecting agriculture. In keeping with the city's entrepreneurial, forward-thinking approach, manufacturing and the service industries have been decentralised leaving the historic centre vibrant and liveable, yet well preserved.

Contemporary Bologna is not without the social challenges and high unemployment which confront other cities of Italy (the Italian youth unemployment rate stands just under 40

A MEDIEVAL MANHATTAN

In medieval times Bologna bristled with over 100 towers. Built by Bolognese nobles these varied in height between 20 metres (65ft) and 60 metres (197ft), with rival families striving to see who could build the highest. But by the 16th century the *torri* had fallen out of fashion. Fire and the fear of collapse were constant hazards, and the great palazzi took over as the main status symbols of noble families. In the late 19th century, during urban regeneration, many of the surviving towers were demolished. Most of the remaining ones tend to tilt, often at alarming angles. Alongside the Cattedrale di San Pietro the Azzoguidi tower, also called Altabella (the Tall Beauty), is the only one standing perfectly vertical. The most famous towers however, and symbols of the city, are the Asinelli and the Garisenda, the 'Twin Towers'. You can climb 498 steps to the top of the Asinelli. Or if you fancy having a tower all to yourself book into the Torre Prendiparte (see page 139). Be warned though, the price – and the climb to the top – are not for the faint-hearted.

Inside the Palazzo d'Accursio

percent at the time of writing). But this is a city that knows how to thrive, and as the capital of one of the richest regions in Europe with the third highest GDP per capita in Italy it is consistently ranked among the top Italian cities for quality of life. It looks after its cultural legacy too. Recent years have seen major restoration of monuments within the historic centre, and the opening or reopening of eight buildings, mainly churches and palaces, which have been recovered by the Fondazione Cassa di Risparmio in Bologna and now form part of a cultural itinerary. A further incentive for visitors is the city location at a major rail hub, making it the perfect springboard for day or half-day trips to the art-filled cities of Emilia Romagna. Modena, which is the home of Pavarotti, Maserati and Ferrari as well as a superlative Duomo, is a mere half-an-hour trip by train; gourmet Parma is less than an hour away. Closer to Bologna, and providing respite from the city streets in summer, are the Colli Bolognesi, the wooded hills of southern Bologna: the first foothills of the verdant Apennines.

Bologna has many facets: a city of history, expressed in every tower and portico, a city of culture and museums, musicians and artists, a top university city, a city of gastronomy and a city of business and trade. But above all this is a city where everything is harmonious, and the cult of beauty permeates most aspects of life. 'La Rossa' notwithstanding, Bologna remains a paradigm of the good life: a citadel of good taste set in the proverbial land of plenty.

A BRIEF HISTORY

Bologna's location, strategically sited between northern and central-southern Italy, has been both a curse and a blessing. The Bolognesi haven't enjoyed many centuries of peace but the various powers that coveted and ruled over the centuries left behind a heady mix of culture and riches. Despite invasions, sieges and plagues, as well as devastation in World War II, Bologna has managed to emerge as one of Italy's wealthiest and most dynamic cities. Its history goes back to a pre-Etruscan civilisation, but it is the medieval period, when a red-brick turreted town grew up around Europe's oldest university, that truly defines the city.

EARLY SETTLERS

As the Bronze Age merged into the Iron Age in around the 9th century BC, northern and central Italy were occupied by

Carving depicting early students at the university

the Villanovian civilisation, named after a site discovered at Villanova just outside Bologna in 1859. This gave way in the 6th century to an Etruscan settlement, called Felsina, on the area where Bologna is today. The town flourished as a trading centre thanks to its link to the port of Spina on the Po Delta. It was a period of peace and prosperity and by the 8th century the Etruscans were dominating the entire region. Displays in Bologna's Archaeological Museum, including grave goods, exquisite statuettes and jewellery, give an insight into the affluence and sophistication of the Etruscan culture.

At the start of the 4th century Etruscan Bologna underwent radical upheaval, with successive waves of invasions by the Celts from over the Alps.

Bologna's Due Torri (Two Towers)

The tribes occupied large stretches of Italy, north of the Apennines and the Marches region. It was one of these tribes, the Boii, which gave the name Bononia to the settlement when it came under Roman control in 189BC.

By this time the Romans had conquered Cisalpine Gaul and set up colonies in the fertile Po Plain. They had built the Via Flaminia, stretching from the Adriatic coast over the Apennines to Rome, and in 187BC completed the long straight Via Aemilia (Emilia), running from Rimini on the east coast to Piacenza, through their newly conquered territories. This established Bononia as a key centre, linking up with the Via Flaminia and hence giving direct military and trading access from Rome. The settlement was substantially rebuilt and extended and although much of Roman Bologna is overlaid by the medieval city, Roman street plans are still visible and the route of the old Via Emilia cuts right through the centre. There are also Roman remains in the Archaeological Museum and in churches where Roman capitals were recycled and incorporated into medieval columns in surprisingly harmonious ways.

HUNS, GOTHS AND LOMBARDS

In the early 5th century the region fell prey to barbaric invaders emigrating south, with invasions from Visigoths and Huns. Despite the incursions a strong Roman Christian culture prevailed. The close relationship between Ambrogio, the Archbishop of Milan, and the Bolognese Bishop, Petronius, who later became the patron saint of the city, enabled the construction of the first wall around the city and the addition of 'holy protection' in the form of four crosses set outside the walls.

Ravenna, a relatively unknown provincial town surrounded by swampland, took centre stage when Honorius, last Emperor of Rome, made it capital of the Western Roman Empire in 404. With the fall of the Western Roman Empire in 476 it came under Gothic rule, like the rest of Italy, but enjoyed a period of recovery and became a rich and powerful city, famous for its glittering early Christian and Byzantine mosaics.

The Lombard King Liutprand captured Bologna in 727. Less than 50 years later the Lombards in turn were ousted by the Franks under Charlemagne who restored the city to the papacy. The city's most ancient churches date back to this era.

The exquisite porticoes of Via Farini

COMMUNES AND DYNASTIC POWERS

In the 11th and 12th centuries Bologna succeeded in wresting itself from Ravenna, whose archbishops controlled the region. It was now free to enjoy the status of an independent commune – or free city state, thus ensuring considerable political and economic autonomy. The University of Bologna, which is now recognised as the oldest in Europe, was founded in 1088 and brought international renown to the city (see box). It was a period of major development too, with the creation of elegant porticoes and high-rise towers, built for wealthy families. Less evident today are the canals which served the watermills to power the textile industries, especially silk. The waterways were also used for ships carrying cargo as trade expanded. By 1200 Bologna had a population of around 50,000 and was one of the great cities of Europe.

But as in the rest of Italy it was also a time of factional strife. The city was one of the main cities of the Lombard League (1167), a medieval alliance of North Italian communes against Emperor Frederick I Barbarossa. There were constant struggles between the Guelphs, supporters of the free cities and the pope, and the pro-Holy Roman Empire Ghibellines. The Guelphs faught constantly with Ghibelline Modena and won a victory against them at the Battle of Fossalta in 1249. The son of Emperor Frederick II, known as Enzo of Sardinia, was captured and imprisoned in Bologna's Palazzo di Re Enzo until his death in 1273.

Internal power struggles led to the decline of the communes and the rise of the region's great family dynasties, ranging from semi-feudal lordships to fully fledged dukedoms and courts of European renown. Throughout the 15th century Bologna was governed by the mighty Bentivoglio family, who produced five successive leaders, and introduced an enlightened regime, bringing in the printing press and embarking on a building programme.

In the region as a whole, dynastic rule was elevated to a way of life, with the noble courts becoming noted centres

BOLOGNA 'LA DOTTA' ('THE LEARNED')

Medieval Bologna's most significant event was the foundation of Europe's first university, believed to have been in 1088. For the first 470 or so years of its existence the university had no fixed location and lectures were held in public buildings or convent halls scattered around the city. Under Pius IV the Palazzo Archiginnasio (see page 38) was built in the city centre in 1562 and this served as the seat of the university until 1803 when it moved permanently to its present premises on Via Zamboni. The prestige of the law school made the city a European centre of scholarship which drew the finest minds of the day. Bologna also developed one of Europe's earliest medical schools and acquired a reputation for scientific research that survives to this day. Palazzo Poggi, the present-day seat of the university, is home to many of its faculties, the university library and a cluster of museums, including some fascinating scientific collections that were used for teaching in former times. The university remains one of the country's finest academic institutions and boasts some of the loveliest university buildings in the country.

Pope Clement VII and Charles V arriving in Bologna for Charles's coronation

of culture, from the Farnese dynasty in Parma to the d'Este dukes in Ferrara, and the Malatesta lords in Rimini. During the Renaissance the ducal courts, especially that of the d'Este, became cultural and artistic centres attracting the finest artists.

CENTURIES OF PAPAL DOMINATION

Bologna's role as a prestigious centre of learning had helped make the city one of the richest, most important and densely populated in Europe. Such prosperity and independence presented a threat to papal power, so the city was annexed by the Papal States in 1506 when Pope Julius besieged Bologna. A year later, encouraged by the papacy, the Bolognesi sacked the monumental palace of the now fallen-from-favour Bentivoglios. Following Bologna, Parma and Piacenza were later annexed by the Papal States and the papal dynasty ended one of the most enlightened Renaissance city-states when it swallowed up Ferrara in

1598 and the remains of the d'Este dukedom transferred to Modena.

The life of Bologna as part of the Papal States was to endure for almost three centuries. When Charles V was crowned Holy Roman Emperor by the pope in 1530 he chose to have the coronation in Bologna's Basilica of San Petronio. His troops had sacked Rome three years earlier and Bologna by this stage enjoyed an importance second only to the capital of the Papal States. It was a double coronation for Charles was also crowned King of Italy in the Palazzo Pubblico (now the Palazzo Comunale). The combined event was chronicled as the 'Triumph of Bologna' for the pomp and splendour of the ceremonies. The following few months saw fervent construction in the city, the papacy showcasing its power and influence through symbolic triumphal arches, classical architecture and statues.

The last decades of the 16th century saw the school of Bolognese painters flourish under the Carraccis, the family of artists who challenged the affectations of Mannerism and satisfied the desire of the Counter-Reformation for a new religious art of simplicity and clarity with a direct appeal to the emotions. Guido Reni, who trained with the Carracci, became one of the greatest painters of the 17th century. But while Bologna was a major art centre and saw the rise of new churches, monasteries and palazzi, it was otherwise a period of political and intellectual stagnation, dominated by the reactionary reforms of the Counter Reformation.

FOREIGN INTERVENTION

Papal rule was interrupted briefly with Napoleonic troops sweeping into Italy in 1796. Bologna, Ferrara, Mantua and Reggio Emilia formed the Cispadane Republic, later to be amalgamated in to the short-lived Cisalpine Republic with

Milan as its capital. The French, who were welcomed in Bologna, made improvements to the city, such as the ring road outside the city walls and the transfer of the University from the Archiginnasio to Palazzo Poggi.

Under the Congress of Vienna in 1815, following the defeat of Napoleon, Bologna was returned to the Papal States. But real control of much of northern Italy rested with reactionary Austria whose troops garrisoned the city from 1815. Insurrections spread through Bologna, Modena and Parma, starting in 1831. Austrian rule finally came to an end when Camillo Cavour, the architect of Italian Unification, decided the only way of defeating Austria was with the support of France. In 1859 the troops of Vittorio Emanuele and Napoleon III of France defeated the Austrians at Magenta and Solferino. The following year the citizens of Bologna voted to become part of the Kingdom of Savoy, which was to become the Kingdom of Italy in 1861.

WORLD WAR II

The 19th century saw Bologna rehearsing its future role, as a radical socialist city in a left-leaning region within the broad 'red belt' of central Italy. Even so, the city flirted with Fascism during the period between the two world wars, and paid the price in 1943–5. The Emilian Apennines marked the Nazis' Gothic Line, making Bologna a strategic target for Allied attacks. The aerial bombardments wreaked havoc on the city, destroying or severely damaging over 40 percent of the buildings in the historic centre.

The bourgeoisie and the land-owning classes succumbed to Fascism, but during the last days of the war, partisans from the area provided the fiercest resistance to Nazi occupation. The Bologna hinterland also suffered Italy's worst Nazi atrocity against civilians. In 1944 the Marzabotto massacre of 1,830 civilians and partisans in the Apennines, south of Bologna, spurred widespread condemnation, as did the Nazi deportation of Jews from Ferrara and Bologna.

MODERN BOLOGNA

In 1945 the city elected a Communist administration and never really looked back. The administration mutated into a left-wing coalition and over the next 50 years imposed an individualistic, modern vision on the city. Bologna became one of the first cities to show that there was no contradiction between a left-wing council and capitalism with a human face. It privatised key social services and encouraged public-private partnership. A bastion of social democracy, civil rights and communal culture, the city pioneered pedestrian precincts, conservation areas, communal housing, gay rights and affordable childcare, as well as sheltered housing for the elderly and student facilities.

But the city of good governance was not without its fair share of the turbulence in Italy during the late 1960s and 1970s. Over a decade of political crime and violent clashes culminated in the 'Bologna Massacre' on 2nd August 1980, when a bomb

The Civil Guard, established in Bologna in 1847

Museum of Modern Art of Bologna (MAMbo)

attributed to a Fascist terrorist organisation ripped through a waiting room of Bologna's Central Station leaving 85 dead and 200 wounded. A gash in the wall and the station clock, permanently fixed at 10.25am, the exact time of the explosion, commemorate the event.

To the dismay of local leftists the long line of left-wing mayors was broken when a centre-right coalition won the elections in 1999, headed by Giorgio Guazzaloca, a conservative businessmen and President of the Chamber of Commerce. In 2004 the left came back to power and has kept it ever since. The last mayor, centre-left Flavio Delbono resigned after 7 months at his post following his involvement in a corruption scandal and was replaced by Virginio Merola in 2011. In recent years Bologna's red reputation has been fading to pink with an increasingly right-wing municipal government.

Bologna has a thriving industrial sector, with emphasis on engineering, electronics, machinery and automobiles. The Fiera is one of the largest exhibition centres in Europe, hosting around 30 international events annually, with themes ranging from construction and packaging to cosmetics and fashion. Like the rest of the country Bologna has suffered from the economic downturn in recent years but continues to retain its place among the top Italian cities for quality of life, wealth and welfare.

HISTORICAL LANDMARKS

9th century BC Villanovan civilisation emerges near Bologna.

4–5th century BC Etruscan settlements in Felsina (Bologna).

189BC Foundation of Roman Bologna (called Bononia).

AD402 Ravenna proclaimed capital of the Western Roman Empire.

476 Ravenna conquered, marking the fall of the Western Roman Empire.

751 End of Byzantine domination in northern Italy.

1088 Foundation of Bologna University, the oldest in Europe.

1167 Bologna joins the Lombard League, an alliance of self-governing republics to defeat Emperor Barbarossa.

1374 Bologna's city walls completed.

1460–1506 Bologna ruled by the local Bentivoglio lords.

1506 Bologna annexed by the Papal States.

1629–31 Bologna loses 15,000 citizens in the plague of 1629–31.

1797–1802 The city becomes part of the Napoleonic Cisalpine Republic.

1815 Bologna and Emilia restored to the Papal States.

1871 Italian Unification.

1915 Italy joins the World War I Allies.

1940 Italy enters World War II as an ally of Nazi Germany.

1943–5 Bologna bombed by the Allies.

1945–1999 Bologna has an uninterrupted string of left-wing mayors.

1980 Fascist terror attack on Bologna Central Station, with 85 deaths.

1982 Italian football team wins World Cup in Spain.

2000 Bologna is European Capital of Culture.

2006 Bologna is named Unesco City of Music.

2010 Centre-left Mayor, Flavio Delbono, resigns after involvement in corruption.

2011 Virginio Merola elected as mayor, leads a left-wing coalition. Bologna ranked 1st out of 107 Italian cities for quality of life.

2012 20 May: Earthquake and aftershocks in Emilia-Romagna leave 26 dead, 20,000 homeless. The Genus Bononiae cultural, artistic and museum itinerary opens in the historic centre.

2016 Celebrations mark the 900th anniversary of the founding of the city.

WHERE TO GO

Bologna is the perfect place to explore on foot. Almost all of the cultural attractions are packed into the historic centre, a large part of which is a Limited Traffic Zone, where traffic is restricted from 7am to 8pm. Furthermore the city is flat and the pavements are protected by arcades. From Piazza Maggiore and from the hub around the famous two towers, streets fan out towards the city gates and the *viali*, the circle of avenues which follows the ancient walls. Via dell'Indipendenza links the rail and bus stations to Piazza Maggiore, and at its southern end forms a T with Via Ugo Bassi running west and Via Rizzo running east. These three main arteries, which are Bologna's high streets, are completely vehicle-free at weekends.

PIAZZA MAGGIORE AND AROUND

Piazza Maggiore and its antechamber, Piazza del Nettuno, form the symbolic heart of the city, showcasing the political and religious institutions that define independent-minded Bologna. Overlooked by brick-built palazzi and the vast mass of San Petronio the sweeping Piazza Maggiore was (and to a certain extent still is) the stage setting where Bolognesi gathered for speeches, ceremonies, meetings and protests. The square is also a showcase for daily life, from Prada-clad beauties to protesting students, pot-bellied sausage-makers to perennially flirtatious pensioners. Just off the piazza the labyrinthine food market provides culinary diversion and the porticoes shelter some of the city's most exclusive shops.

PIAZZA DEL NETTUNO

The focus of the piazza is ***Fontana del Nettuno*** ❶, the celebrated bronze fountain to Neptune sculpted by Giambologna in

Fontana del Nettuno is a popular meeting point

The Maserati connection

Motoring enthusiasts may recognise Neptune's trident in the *Fontana del Nettuno*. It was adopted by the Modena-based Maserati car company as their logo.

1556. An Italian in all but birth (he was born Jean Boulogne in Flanders) the Mannerist sculptor spent most of his working life in Florence but it was the *Fountain of Neptune* in Bologna which made his name. The sculpture depicts a monumental, muscle-bound Neptune (nicknamed 'Il Gigante') with four *putti*, representing the winds, and four voluptuous sirens who sit astride dolphins, spouting water from their nipples. Given Bologna's turbulent relationship with the papacy, the citizens delighted in the fact that the nude Neptune was considered a profane, pagan symbol by the papal authorities. The statue caused a furore when first unveiled and a Counter-Reformation edict decreed that Neptune should be robed. But the priapic sea god is now free to frolic. (Locals take great delight in pointing out the best vantage point for viewing the god's impressive manhood).

PALAZZO DI RE ENZO AND PALAZZO DEL PODESTÀ

Facing the fountain, on the east side of the square, stands **Palazzo Re Enzo** (access only during exhibitions), named after the son of Emperor Frederick II, Enzo 'King of Sardinia', who was defeated by the Guelphs versus Ghibellines Battle of Fossalta in 1249 and was imprisoned here for 23 years until his death in 1272. Adjoining the palace and facing Piazza Maggiore is the elegant **Palazzo del Podestà** (access only during exhibitions), built as the political seat of power in the 13th century. It is graced by a Renaissance porticoed facade on the Piazza Maggiore side and distinguished by its 13th-century brick tower, the Torre dell'Arengo, originally built to summon citizens in case of emergency. The vault below, the Voltone del

Podesta, was once occupied by terracotta statues of the town's patron saints. The attraction today is the echo in the 'whispering gallery' – face one of the four corners of the arcade and your voice will be transmitted to the opposite corner.

The wall on the west side of Piazza del Nettuno features photos of hundreds of partisans who fought for the Resistance in World War II. Of the 14,425 local partisans, including over 2,000 women, 2,059 died. Italy was liberated from Nazi domination on 21st April 1945 by which time Bologna had been devastated by aerial bombardments. A further memorial honours the victims of the bomb explosion at Bologna's main railway station in 1980 which left 85 dead and 200 wounded.

PALAZZO D'ACCURSIO

The vast and imposing building on the west side of Piazza Maggiore is the **Palazzo d'Accursio**, also known as the

The porticoed Palazzo del Podestà

Palazzo Comunale, the medieval town hall remodelled in the Renaissance

Palazzo Comunale ❷ (www.museibologna.it/arteantica; Tue–Fri 9am–6.30pm, Sat–Sun 10am–6.30pm, some ceremonial halls open Tue–Sun 10am–1pm if not being used for council meetings; charge only for the Collezioni Comunali d'Arte, the Municipal Art Collection). The palace dates back to the 13th century and was originally the residence of a well-known medieval lawyer, Accursius. It was later bought by the city and remodelled as an affirmation of papal authority. In 1530, two days before he was crowned Emperor in San Petronio, Charles V was crowned King of Italy in the chapel of the Palazzo d'Accursio, receiving the Iron Cross of Lombardy. A suspended passage was built especially for the occasion, linking the palace to San Petronio across Piazza Maggiore.

The huge bronze statue (1580) above the portal of the palace depicts Pope Gregory XIII, the Bolognese pope who reformed the old Roman calendar, replacing it with his own Gregorian one, still in use today. Above and to the left of the doorway is a beautiful terracotta statue of the *Virgin and Child* (1478) by the Italian sculptor Niccolò dell'Arca. Cross the courtyard and climb the magnificent corded staircases, where horses once thundered past, to the frescoed interiors on the first and second floors. Restyled by papal legates in the

16th century, the **ceremonial halls** are elaborately frescoed and have fine views over Piazza Maggiore. The Sala Rossa, or Red Room, with its huge chandeliers, is a favourite venue for civil ceremonies. The Museo Morandi which opened here in 1993 was moved to MAMbo (see page 64) in 2012 while this part of the palace was restored. The museum will return here after the work is complete (2019 is the aim). The many rooms of the **Collezioni Comunali d'Art** at the top of the palace display Emilian works of art from the 13th to 19th centuries, worth visiting for a sense of the decor, furnishings and artistic taste under papal rule, rather than for great art.

SALABORSA

Part of the monumental Palazzo Comunale complex, the **Biblioteca Salaborsa** (Tue–Fri 10am–8pm, Sat 10am–7pm; free) was built within the shell of the former Stock Exchange (Borsa). The building is now a spacious multimedia library and cultural space, designed in art nouveau style. A glass floor in the Covered Square reveals excavations of the medieval and Roman settlements including part of the forum and Roman pavement, and these can be accessed from the lower basement level (Tue–Sat 10am–1.30pm and 3–6.30pm; free).

Before its current role, this sizeable section of the Palazzo Comunale served diverse purposes. In 1568 the Bolognese naturalist, Ulisse Aldrovandi, founded Bologna's Botanic Garden in the courtyard here for the academic study of medicinal plants. This was one of the first botanic gardens in Europe (Bologna's botanic garden today is in the university quarter). The courtyard later became a training ground for the military, then in the 20th century served variously as bank offices, a puppet theatre and a basketball ground before becoming the Stock Exchange.

PIAZZA MAGGIORE

A sunny day is a summons to sit at café tables in the **Piazza Maggiore ❸** or on the steps under the arcades and soak up the atmosphere. Dominating the great central square is the vast but incomplete Basilica of San Petronio, favourite church of the Bolognesi. The slightly raised platform in the middle of the piazza is familiarly called the *crescentone* after the name of the local flat bread, *crescente*, which it resembles in shape.

BASILICA DI SAN PETRONIO

Dedicated to Petronius, the city's patron saint, the 14th-century **Basilica di San Petronio ❹** (www.basilicadisan petronio.it; daily 7.45am–1.15pm, 3–6pm; free) is the city's principal church. As one of the most monumental Gothic basilicas in Italy, the church would have been larger than St Peter's in Rome had not Pope Pius IV put a stop to construction by using the funds for the creation of a new university, the Palazzo Archiginnasio. As a consequence the facade was never completed, hence only the partial cladding in pink Verona marble and the cut-off transept which you can see down the alley to the right of the basilica. Even so, San Petronio is still monumental and remains the city's best-loved church, representing a manifestation of civic will rather than religious power. Built over Roman foundations the vaulted church reveals columns recycled from the Augustan era, which meld perfectly with medieval additions.

Bologna Welcome Card

The excellent tourist office on Piazza Maggiore can supply you with a 48-hour Bologna Welcome Card. At €20 it's good value giving you free admission to most city museums, plus two tickets for the airport shuttle bus (BLQ line) and discounts for shops, restaurants and events. Also available at www.bologna welcome.com.

San Petronio's half-completed facade

The highly expressive reliefs on the **Porta Magna**, the central portal, were the last great work of Sienese sculptor Jacopo della Quercia, occupying the last 13 years of his life (1425–38). The architrave displays scenes from the New Testament, and on the two pilasters on either side of the door, dramatic reliefs with subjects taken from the Old Testament. Michelangelo, who visited Bologna in 1494, admired these reliefs and used several of the motifs (such as *The Creation of Adam*) for the Sistine Ceiling. The lunette features the *Madonna and Child* between St Petronius and St Ambrose.

The immense but simple interior of the basilica has witnessed historical events, not least of which was the crowning of Charles V as Holy Roman Emperor in 1530 (see page 23). Set in the floor on the left is a 17th-century sundial, measuring almost 60m (197ft) and said to be the world's biggest church sundial. It was of particular interest to travellers on the Grand Tour and today it still attracts plenty of interest, especially at noon on a sunny day when rays touch the line of the sundial.

Madonna and Child above the altar

The second chapel on the left is dedicated to San Petronio and contains the relics of the saint. The **Bolognini Chapel** (4th on the left) remains virtually intact, and has striking early 15th-century frescoes by Giovanni da Modena, depicting the *Journey of the Magi*, *the Life of St Petronius*, *Paradise* and a harrowing scene of the *Last Judgement*. There are 20 more chapels, an organ to the right of the altar, dating from 1470 and still functioning (the one opposite still works too but is relatively modern at 1596), and a museum with projects for the completion of the facade which were never carried through.

During the ongoing major renovations to the south side of the cathedral (likely to carry on until 2019) visitors can take the scaffolding lift or steps up to the **panoramic terrace** (access from Piazza Galvani). From here there are splendid views of the cityscape and the Apennine hills to the south.

MUSEO CIVICO ARCHEOLOGICO

From Piazza Maggiore the Via Archiginnasio takes you under the porticoes past the city's most elegant shops, including the loveliest arcades, known as the Pavaglione. The **Museo Civico Archeologico** ❺ (www.museibologna.it/archeologico; Tue–Fri 9am–3pm, Sat–Sun 10am–6.30pm; opening times may be extended during temporary exhibitions) is housed in the former hospital of Santa Maria della Morte (of Death), which was dedicated to the terminally ill. The lovely courtyard is framed by Roman statuary and leads to Giambologna's statue of Neptune which is displayed at the top of the main staircase. Bologna's early history is traced through Celtic tools, Etruscan urns, Attic vases and Classical Greek terracottas, proof that the Bolognese talent for trading dates back to its earliest history. The sheer number of exhibits – around 200,000 – in old-fashioned dimly-lit galleries can be overwhelming but the museum has one of the best Etruscan collections in Italy. Two large galleries are devoted to the Etruscan civilisation in Bologna (9th–4th centuries BC), featuring terracotta and bronze ossuaries, funerary stelae with depictions of fantastic animals and exquisite terracotta askos (small vessels for pouring liquids). There are also good displays of Roman antiquities and (easy to miss) an impressive Egyptian collection in the basement.

CITY OF PORTICOES

A distinctive feature of the city are the *portici,* or porticoes, extending almost 40km (25 miles). These graceful, tranquil arcades were originally built of wood outside shopkeepers' houses as extra space for trade. The original portico had to be a minimum of 7 'Bolognese feet' high (2.66m) to enable those on horseback to pass through. From 1568, due mainly to fire hazards, porticoes had to be made of brick or stone. A few of the old wooden ones survive and one of the best preserved examples is the lofty portico of Casa Isolani in Strada Maggiore. The Portico San Luca, running for nearly 3.5km (2 miles) up to the hilltop Sanctuary of San Luca, is the longest portico in the world. Over the centuries the porticoes have been much admired by travellers both for their architectural interest and their protection against the elements. In a city renowned for rain and snow in winter, and searing heat in mid-summer, they couldn't be more convenient.

PALAZZO DELL'ARCHIGINNASIO

Just beyond the Archaeological Museum is the cultural set-piece of the frescoed **Palazzo dell'Archiginnasio ❻**, built in 1562–3 as the first permanent seat of Europe's most ancient university (www.archiginnasio.it; Palace Courtyard and open gallery: Mon–Fri 10am–6pm, Sat 10am–7pm, Sun 10am–2pm, free; Anatomical Theatre and Stabat Mater Hall: Mon–Fri 10am–6pm, Sat 10am–7pm, Sun and hols 10am–2pm, if not occupied by events). Before the construction of the Archiginnasio the schools of law and medicine had been scattered around various venues of the city. This remained the seat of the university until 1803 when it moved to its current location in Via Zamboni. Today the palace houses the precious collection of 800,000 works of the Biblioteca Comunale (City Library), the richly decorated Sala dello Stabat Mater, a former lecture hall where Rossini's first Italian performance of *Stabat Mater* was held in 1842 under the direction of Donizetti, and the fascinating Teatro Anatomico (Anatomy Theatre).

The fine courtyard, with its double loggia, and the staircase and halls are all decorated by memorials commemorating masters of the ancient university together with around 6,000 student coats of arms. The courtyard was frequently the scene of university ceremonies, one of the most intriguing being the Preparation of the Teriaca (Theriac), a drug for animal bites and later the all-cure medicine, formulated by the Greeks in 1st century AD and concocted from fermented herbs, poisons, animal flesh, honey and numerous other ingredients.

Some of the first human dissections in Europe were performed in the **Teatro Anatomico**, shaped like an amphitheatre and adorned with wooden statues of famous university anatomists of the university and celebrated doctors. There is nothing remotely macabre about the tiered seats and professors' chair – apart from a canopy supported by depictions of a couple of skinned cadavers, *gli spellati*. The Church forbade regular sessions of dissections but when they did take place they were popular events, open to the public. As photos at the entrance illustrate, this wing of the building was devastated during the bombardment of 1944, but was reconstructed immediately after the war, using the original wooden sculptures that were salvaged from the rubble.

The Via dell'Archiginnasio leads into **Piazza Galvani**, named after the 18th-century Bolognese scientist Luigi Galvani, pioneer of bioelectromagnetics. Through his experiments on frogs he established that bioelectric forces exist within animal tissue. The statue in the square shows Galvani gazing at a frog on a stone slab. For a break from sightseeing head to Zanarini on the corner of the Piazza, a great spot for coffee and cakes.

Legendary Tamburini deli

QUADRILATERO

The maze of alleys tucked away off Piazza Maggiore is known as the Quadrilatero. It is an ancient grid of food shops where the mood is as boisterous as it was in its medieval heyday. The ancient guilds of the city, such as goldsmiths, blacksmiths, butchers, fishmongers and furriers had their headquarters here and many eet names today recall their trades. The market place for a true taste of Emilia, with open-air stalls, specialised food shops and a covered market, **Mercato di Mezzo ❼**, now transformed into a stylish food hall selling enticing regional produce and a wide range of freshly made tapas-style snacks to take away or eat in, very casually, at communal tables. From here the market spills out onto Via Drapperie, Via Clavature and Via degli Orefici. Gaze and graze is the mantra of most visitors. On offer are juicy peaches and cherries, sculpted pastries, navel-shaped handmade pasta, slivers of delicious pink Parma ham, succulent Bolognese Mortadella, still-wriggling seafood and wedges of superior 'black rind' parmesan.

By day, few people can resist lunch at **Tamburini** (Via Drapperie/Via Caprarie 1), the legendary gourmet deli with a self service, followed perhaps by a delicious pastry at **Atti** (Via Drapperie 6); or a picnic of charcuterie from **Salumeria Simoni** (Via Drapperie 5/2A), where whole hams hang from

WHERE TIME STANDS STILL

Only the word 'Vino' above the doorway hints that you might have arrived at an inn. The inconspicuous Osteria del Sole, just off Via Pescheria at Vicolo Ranocchi 1/D (www.osteriadelsole.it) is Bologna's oldest inn, dating from 1465. It's an atmospheric, rough-and-ready spot, with old framed photos on the walls, cheap wine served by the glass and long tables for customers to bring their own food – which they have done for centuries. Pick up a picnic from the market stalls or from neighbouring delis, order your glass of Sangiovese or Pignoletto and sit with cheerful old boys playing cards, students from the university or the occasional tourist who has managed to locate this elusive inn.

the ceiling and wheels of cheeses and thick rolls of Mortadella are crammed into the windows. In the evening the Quadrilatero becomes a chic spot for an *aperitivo* in an outdoor café.

Lamentation over the Dead Christ

SANTA MARIA DELLA VITA

After the bustle of the surrounding market the church of **Santa Maria della Vita** ❽ (Via Clavature 8; www.genusbononiae.it; Tue–Sun 10.30am–6.30pm) is a haven of peace. Although boldly frescoed the restored baroque interior is overshadowed by the *Lamentation over the Dead Christ* (1463) by Niccolò dell'Arca, a remarkable composition in terracotta portraying life-size grieving mourners at the death of Christ. The church was part of a religious hospital complex and it is thought that Niccolò dell'Arca may well have studied the faces of the sick and suffering to have achieved such stunning expressions of grief. The figure of Nicodemus is traditionally described as a self-portrait. In the oratory, where temporary exhibitions are held, there is another poignant lament in terracotta, the *Death of the Virgin*, by Alfonso Lombardi.

EAST OF PIAZZA MAGGIORE

With its long rows of noble palazzi and secret courtyards, the east side of the medieval city has always been the most fashionable quarter of the city. The Strada Maggiore follows the route of the Roman Via Emilia which linked with the Via Flaminia – the route to Rome. The porticoed street is lined by a succession of senatorial palazzi which once belonged to ruling families. To the north, Via San Vitale was formerly called Via Salaria, for it was along here that salt was transported into the city from the Cervia salt flats south of Ravenna. Via Santo Stefano, the ancient road to Tuscany, is flanked by yet more fine mansions and leads to, and beyond, the beguiling complex of Santo Stefano.

DUE TORRI

Dominating Piazza di Porta Ravegnana, site of the main gate of the Roman walls, are the **Due Torri ❾**, the Two Towers. The **Torre degli Asinelli** (daily Apr–Sep 9am–6pm, Oct–Mar 9am–5pm) and the **Torre Garisenda** (no access) are the most potent symbols of the medieval era, when Bologna bristled with around 120 towers. Both date back to the 12th century, and were probably built as watchtowers as well as status symbols. Legend has it that the two richest families in

The view over the sea of red rooftops from the Torre degli Asinelli

Bologna, the Asinelli and the Garisenda, competed to build the tallest and most beautiful tower in the city.

A sense of history and a bird's eye view over the terracotta rooftops should tempt you to the top of Torre degli Asinelli (over 97m/ 318ft). It is admittedly a steep climb, with a narrow spiral

staircase of 498 steps, but worth the effort. From the top you can locate some of the other 20-odd surviving medieval towers and, weather permitting, the foothills of the Alps beyond Verona. Like most of Bologna's towers, the Due Torri are both tilting: Garisenda 3.33m (11ft) to the northeast, Asinelli 2.23m (7.3ft) to the west. Garisenda originally rose to 60m (197ft) but it was built on weak foundations, and for safety reasons 12m (39ft) was lopped off in the mid-14th century. From certain angles, however, the two towers appear to be the same height. Dante, who was briefly in Bologna during his exile from Florence, and saw the acutely tilting tower (before it was shortened), included it in *The Inferno*, where he compares it to the bending Antaeus, giant son of Poseidon, frozen in ice at the bottom of hell. His quote is engraved on a plaque at the base of the tower.

Below the towers, but in no way inconspicuous, is the 17th-century church of **San Bartolomeo**, with a Renaissance portico. Look for the *Annunciation* by Francesco Albani in the fourth chapel of the south aisle, and the small *Madonna with Child* by Guido Reni in the north transept. On the north side of the square the intrusion of a starkly modern office building invariably caused a furore when constructed in the 1950s.

Palazzo della Mercanzia

PIAZZA DELLA MERCANZIA

Heart of the commercial district since medieval times, **Piazza della Mercanzia** ⑩ is dominated by the crenellated **Palazzo della Mercanzia**, formerly the merchants' exchange and customs house, now seat of Bologna's Chamber of Commerce. The Gothic facade is adorned by statues representing the city's patron saints who smile benignly on an economy once based on gold, textiles, silk and hemp, but now in thrall to local success stories such as silky La Perla lingerie, hemp-free Bruno Magli shoes and Mandarina Duck bags. The palace safeguards the original recipes of local specialities, such as Bolognese *tagliatelle al ragù* (with the real Bolognese sauce). Pappagallo (see page 109), a charming old-world institution in a beautiful 13th-century building on the piazza, is a good place to try it.

STRADA MAGGIORE

Running southeast from Piazza Mercanzia is **Strada Maggiore** or Main Street, with an almost uninterrupted succession of aristocratic residences. On the left-hand side, at No 26, is the **Casa Rossini** ⑪, the composer's home from 1829 and 1848. Just beyond it on the right is the lofty and quaintly porticoed **Casa Isolani**, one of the city's few surviving 13th-century houses. Beyond it the **Caffè Commercianti** (No 23c) is traditionally favoured by academic types including the late polymath and best-selling author, Umberto Eco. Modelled on a Parisian café, it has Art Deco and art nouveau touches, and makes a chic coffee or cocktail stop.

MUSEO INTERNAZIONALE E BIBLIOTECA DELLA MUSICA

A mere baton's throw from Rossini's home, the Palazzo Sanguinetti at No 34 Strada Maggiore is home to the delightful **Museo Internazionale e Biblioteca della Musica** ⑫ (International Museum and Library of Music; www.musei bologna.it/musica; Tue–Fri 9.30am–4pm, Sat–Sun 10am–6.30pm). Rossini and his second wife, Olimpia Pelissier, were hosted here by their tenor friend, Domenico Donzelli. The museum is a recognition of Bologna's musical status: nine rooms trace six centuries of European music through 80 rare and antique musical instruments along with scores, historical documents and portraits. Even those who are not fans of classical music will be entranced by the *trompe-l'œil* courtyard and the frescoed interiors, offering a rare chance to see

MOZART AND MARTINI

In Room 3 of the Museum of Music you can find memorabilia of the young Mozart including two versions of his entrance exam to the Accademia Filarmonica di Bologna. His written test did not comply with the strict academic rules, so Father Giambattista Martini, who had taught Mozart and recognised his genius, secretly handed him the correct version. The museum has two versions of his test below his portrait, one of which includes several mistakes. Mozart came to Bologna twice in 1770 when he was 14. On the first occasion he performed a private concert for Count Pallavicini in his palace in Via San Felice and stayed at the Albergo del Pellegrino, which no longer exists.

how the Bolognese nobility lived. The salon-like atmosphere, reflected in the mythological friezes and whimsical pastoral scenes, makes this the most enchanting city palace. The music library, with over 100,000 volumes opened here in 2014, after its transfer from Piazza Rossini.

MUSEO CIVICO D'ARTE INDUSTRIALE E GALLERIA DAVIA BARGELLINI

Beside the Palazzo Sanguinetti looms the **Torre degli Oseletti**, a medieval tower which was originally 70m (230 ft) tall. At the junction of Strada Maggiore and Piazza Aldrovandi, you are unlikely to miss the 'Palace of the Giants', **Palazzo Davia Bargellini**, whose entrance is flanked by two baroque telamones. The palace is home to the **Museo Civico d'Arte Industriale e Galleria Davia Bargellini ⓭** (www.musei bologna.it/arteantica; Tue–Sat 9am–2pm, Sun 9am–1pm; free), a collection of applied and decorative arts, and notably Bolognese paintings, many of which belonged the Bargellini family who started collecting in 1500. Works include Vitale da Bologna's famous *Madonna dei Denti* (Madonna of the Teeth), a *Pietà* (1368) by his contemporary Simone dei Crocifissi, and the *Giocatori di Dadi* (*The Dice Players*) by Giuseppe Maria Crespi (1740), who specialised in genre scenes with vivid chiaroscuro effects. The last room holds an 18th-century Bolognese puppet theatre.

SANTA MARIA DEI SERVI

Across the road is the lovely Gothic **Santa Maria dei Servi ⓮** (daily 8am–noon 3.30–8pm; free), graced by an elegant portico. Work on the church started in 1346 but it was almost two centuries before completion. The most interesting works of art lie behind the elaborate altar including (on the right side) fragment frescoes on the ceiling by Vitale da Bologna and, in

Gothic Santa Maria dei Servi

a chapel on the left which you have to light up, an *Enthroned Madonna* (1280–90) traditionally attributed to the great Tuscan master Cimabue, but now thought to be from his workshop.

SANTO STEFANO

From Strada Maggiore the **Corte Isolani** ⓯, entered under the portico of Casa Isolani, is a bijou warren that runs into Via Santo Stefano. Gentrification has turned this cluster of medieval palaces into chic art galleries, desirable apartments, wine bars and cafés. **Via Santo Stefano** is every bit as gracious as Strada Maggiore with late Gothic palaces once favoured by Bolognese silk merchants. Regular upward glances often reveal 12th-century tower-houses incorporated in late-medieval residences and embellished with Renaissance facades. **Piazza Santo Stefano** ⓰ is a gentrified neighbourhood square (though more triangular than square), at its most convivial during an antiques market or gourmet food fair. This sought-after quarter numbers the once-radical politician, Romano Prodi, among its ranks – proof, if needed, that politically red Bologna now prefers pale pink.

The cobbled piazza forms the intimate backdrop to **Santo Stefano** ⑰ (daily 8am–7pm; free), the city's most hallowed spot. You will need plenty of time to appreciate and work out this ecclesiastical labyrinth, with its feast of ancient and medieval churches. Originally it was a complex of seven churches in one, as at Jerusalem, and it is known as Le Sette Chiese ('the Seven Churches') despite the fact that only four survive.

The complex dates back at least to the 5th century and may have been founded by Bishop Petronius as his cathedral on the site of a former pagan temple. His corpse was discovered here in 1141. The Lombards established their religious centre here, it then became a Benedictine sanctuary in the 10th century. Santo Stefano is still run by stern Benedictines who only soften when talking of the basilica's enduring appeal. One white-clad brother confides: "Dante often came here to meditate in 1287 but we are not fussy – at Easter even the local prostitutes come here for confession".

A harmonious ensemble is created by the interlocking churches and courtyards, including the Benedictine

Santo Stefano church complex

cloisters, graced by an elegant well head. Seen from the beautiful Piazza Santo Stefano the larger church on the right is the Chiesa del Crocifisso (Church of the Crucifix), the one in the middle the Church of San Sepolcro modelled on Jerusalem's Holy Sepulchre, and on the left Santi Vitale e Agricola, the oldest church in Bologna. Enter through the **Chiesa del Crocifisso**, of Lombard origin but which has undergone the most transformation. The church ends with a central stairway that climbs to the Presbytery. Steps lead down to a graceful little crypt, built to house the relics of the early Bolognese martyrs Vitale and Agricola who died around 304 AD. Their remains are contained in a golden urn on the altar. A door on the left of the main church leads into the most famous of the churches: the **Basilica of San Sepolcro**, a small and unusual polygonal, surrounded by columns, some of which survive from an ancient pagan temple. The body of St Petronius was found in this church in the mid-12th century; his relics used to lie in an urn in the centre of the small chapel but were transferred in 2000 to join the saint's head in the Basilica of San Petronio.

Bathed in mystical light the 11th-century **Santi Vitale e Agricola** is most compelling. Unadorned and built of bare brick it retains the most Romanesque Lombard character of all the churches in the city. It is dedicated to the first Bolognese martyrs, Vitale and Agricola, whose graves were discovered in 393 by the great bishop of Milan, St Ambrose. Adjoining it is the **Cortile di Pilato** (Pilate's Courtyard) a fine brick-walled courtyard with a large marble basin erroneously believed to have been used by Pontius Pilate to wash his hands. Under the arcades are chapels and tombstones. Beyond the courtyard lies the mystery **Martyrium**, a transverse church also named the Holy Cross or Trinity Church. Little is known of its origin and history. As you walk along there are niches that light up, one with a sculpted scene of the *Adoration of the Magi* by the Bolognese artist Simone de' Crocifissi. The courtyard leads into the peaceful Benedictine **cloister**, with two tiers of loggias. In the corner is a tiny museum of early Bolognese paintings and reliquaries, and a shop selling liqueurs and lotions made by Carmelite monks.

THE UNIVERSITY QUARTER

The University of Bologna, founded in the 11th century and famous in its early days for reviving the study of Roman law, is the oldest university in Europe. Petrarch attended classes here, as did Erasmus, Copernicus, various popes and cardinals – and more recently Guglielmo Marconi, Enzo Ferrari and Giorgio Armani. It is ranked the number one university in Italy and today attracts over 80,000 students annually from around the world. The heart of the student area is the triangle between Via Zamboni and Via San Vitale, but the university quarter also spills out onto Via delle Belli Arti. It is one of the most diverse districts, studded with churches, palaces and museums as well as arty bookshops, eclectic cafés, shabby-chic student dives and graffiti-splashed porticos. The curious Palazzo Poggi, sumptuous seat of the University, is home to several of the university's specialist museums and the Pinacoteca Nazionale boasts the richest art collection in the region.

A leisurely stroll down Via Zamboni reveals the faculties of modern languages, philosophy, law, economics and the sciences, with each noble palace telling its own story. On the left, at No. 20, is the senatorial 16th-century **Palazzo Magnani** ⑱; its hall of honour is decorated with a stunning cycle of frescoes depicting the *The Story of the Foundation of Rome* (1592) by the three Carracci painters, Annibale, Agostino and Ludovico. The two brothers and their cousin worked collaboratively in their early careers and it is not easy to work out their individual contributions. The palace is the seat of UniCredit Bank but the frieze can be seen on request – ask at the bank reception or telephone in advance on 051-640 8221.

SAN GIACOMO MAGGIORE

Across the road lies **Piazza Rossini**, named after the composer who studied for three years (1806–9) at the Conservatorio G.B. Martini on the piazza. His first compositions and public performances date from this time, including a historic concert with the opera singer Isabella Colbran whom he married in 1822.

Overlooking the square is the church of **San Giacomo Maggiore** ⑲ (Mon–Fri 7.30am–12.30pm and 3.30–6.30pm, Sat–Sun 8.30am–12.30pm and 3.30–6.30pm; free), known as the Bentivoglio family's church. The Romanesque facade

The ornate Medicine faculty at the university

and portals flanked by lions pre-date Bologna's grandest dynasty but the elegant Renaissance portico dates from their era, as do many of the superb paintings in their family chapel (follow the sign as you enter the church). Although only open on Saturday morning (9.30am–12.30pm) the chapel can be seen through the railings and illuminated by inserting a 50 cent coin. The *Madonna and Child* (1488) and the eerie *Triumph of Death* and *Triumph of Fame* are all by the Ferrarese painter Lorenzo Costa who worked in Bologna before succeeding Mantegna as the principal painter at the Gonzaga court at Mantua. The *Madonna and Child* (the Bentivoglio Altarpiece) features Giovanni il Bentivoglio, his wife and eleven children and was allegedly commissioned in thanksgiving for the family's escape from an attempted massacre by a rival family. The *Madonna and Saints* (1494) by Francesco Raibolini, better known as 'Il Francia', is generally regarded as the best of the artist's many altarpieces.

ORATORIO DI SANTA CECILIA

Lorenzo Costa, Il Francia and contemporaries also worked on the **Oratorio di Santa Cecilia** ⓴ (daily Oct–May 10am–1pm and 3–6pm, Jun–Sep 10am–1pm and 2–7pm; free but donations welcome) which adjoins San Giacomo Maggiore and is accessed via the portico. This little gem was built in 1267 but remodelled by the Bentivoglios who commissioned the artists to portray the *Life and Martyrdom of St Cecilia*, patron saint of music. The lively but little known Renaissance fresco cycle starts with Cecilia's wedding (far left) and ends with her burial (far right). The scenes are accompanied by the bold statement 'the night after her marriage to a pagan youth, Cecilia revealed that she had taken a vow of chastity and persuaded her husband to convert as she was a bride of Christ'. Even so, the bride met a sticky end, boiled alive, then beheaded as portrayed in the gory decapitation scene on the left as you enter. St Cecilia is patron saint of music so it is appropriate that classical concerts (free of charge) are held in the oratory.

Teatro Comunale

PIAZZA VERDI AND TEATRO COMUNALE

Further along Via Zamboni, **Piazza Verdi ㉑** is a hub of student life. Café Scuderia, with tables spilling out onto the square, is all about chilling out over cheap coffee or beer. Music often wafts from the **Teatro Comunale ㉒** (www.comunalebologna.it), the opera house overlooking the square. Originally called the Nuovo Teatro Pubblico, the theatre was built to replace the wooden Teatro Malvezzi destroyed by fire in 1745. In Renaissance times this was the site of the sumptuous, 244-room Palazzo Bentivoglio, which was sacked and destroyed in 1507 by the masses who had become discontented with the rule of the Bentivoglio dynasty. The adjoining Via Guasto (*guasto* meaning 'breakdown' or formerly 'devastation'), and the modern Giardini del Guasto derived their names from the ruins that laid here for decades. The 1930s facade of the Teatro Comunale belies an elegant baroque-style interior with tiers of boxes (no access apart from performances). Many of these were formerly owned by titled families, each

Museum of Human Anatomy exhibits inside the Palazzo Poggi

one individually decorated and bearing the family's coat of arms on the ceiling. The opera house played host to 20 operas by Rossini, who lived for many years in Bologna, as well as historic performances such as the premiere of Gluck's *Il Tronfio di Clelia* and the Italian premiere of Verdi's *Don Carlo* in 1867. It was also receptive to works of composers outside Italy and was the first Italian opera house to stage a Wagner opera, *Lohengrin*, in 1871. Today it is the city's main venue for opera (November to April), classical concerts and ballet.

PALAZZO POGGI

In 1803 the university moved from the Archiginnasio (see page 38) to the 16th-century **Palazzo Poggi** ㉓ (Via Zamboni 33; Tue–Fri 10am–4pm, Sat–Sun 10.30am–5.30pm; charge only for guided visits of the Specola, the Observatory, for which reservations are recommended, tel: 051-209 9360). This opulent seat of the university, decorated with Mannerist and early Baroque frescoes, is home to a confusing yet fascinating cluster of university museums. In the 17th and 18th centuries, this was the leading scientific institute in Europe, based on Bologna's history of scholarship, particularly in anatomy and astronomy. A visit to the **Specola** tower on a guided tour (in Italian and English) is highly recommended; it also includes the Specola Museum and its rich collection of instruments for astronomical studies such as medieval astrolabes and celestial and terrestrial globes. The tower was built on top of the building and served as an astronomical observatory.

The collections in the university served primarily for research rather than as attractions for visitors, but it's worth wandering through the vaulted frescoed galleries, with cycles of 16th-century frescoes, and picking out a few curiosities. Exhibits (many of which now have labels and explanations in English) range from models of military architecture and reconstructions of 17th-century warships to precious manuscripts and Japanese woodcuts. But the invariable magnets are the Museums of Obstetrics and Human Anatomy. Set up for teaching surgeons, doctors and midwives in the 18th century the collection includes a birthing chair on which students would practise blindfold as well as terracotta and wax

MARCONI: BOLOGNA'S WIRELESS PIONEER

Among Bologna University's famous alumni is Guglielmo Marconi (1874–1937), known for his pioneering work on long-distance wireless communication. He was born in Bologna in 1874 to a wealthy Italian landowner and his Irish-Scots wife but when Italy showed no interest in his experiments or requests for funding he moved to the UK. At the age of 27 he succeeded in receiving the first transatlantic radio signal which led to a worldwide revolution in telecommunications. In 1909 Marconi shared the Nobel Prize in Physics for his work on wireless telegraphy. His Marconi Company radios saved hundreds of lives, including the 700 surviving passengers of the sinking *Titanic* in 1912. Bologna's airport was named after him in 1978. Some of Marconi's earliest experiments were completed at the family home, Villa Griffone at Pontechhio Marconi, 15km (9 miles) from Bologna, now home to the Marconi Museum (www.fgm.it; guided tours, reservation only).

models of wrongly-presented foetuses and gruesome models of human dissections.

There is more to see on Via Irnerio to the north of Palazzo Poggi: the university's Botanical Garden, Museum of Physics (currently closed) and the **L. Cattaneo Museo delle Cere Anatomiche** (Museum of Anatomic Wax Models; Mon–Thu 10am–1pm and 2–5pm, Fri 10am–1pm; free) at No 48, with more waxwork teaching aids, including models of faces with small pox and tumours, human intestines and conjoined twins.

PINACOTECA NAZIONALE

Just north of Palazzo Poggi, on Via delle Belle Arti is the **Pinacoteca Nazionale** ㉔ (National Art Gallery; www.pina cotecabologna.beniculturali.it; Tue and Wed 9am–1.30pm, Thu, Fri, Sat, Sun 2–7pm; ticket office closes 30 mins before), the finest treasure house in the city. The National Gallery's

A painting depicting medieval Bologna at the Pinacoteca Nazionale.

only flaw is its tendency to close sections for 'lack of personnel'. Created during the Napoleonic occupation, the museum displays paintings plucked from demolished or deconsecrated churches. As was his wont

Wise words

"When Bologna stops teaching, Bologna will be no more". The words of the Archdeacon of Bologna's cathedral and head chancellor of the Studium (University) in 1687.

Napoleon stole many of the finest treasures for the Louvre but Bologna managed to get them back in 1815. The gallery follows the path of Bolognese and Emilian art from the Middle Ages to the 18th century, but also includes works by artists from Florence, Tuscany and other 'foreign' parts, showing the influence on local artists.

The itinerary begins with works by Bolognese artists of the 14th century, and notably the vigorous and brilliantly coloured *St George and the Dragon* (c.1335) by Vitale da Bologna. Though cast in Byzantine-influenced Gothic mould, this dramatic, stylised scene shows the realism and expressiveness typical of Trecento Bolognese art. Other gallery scene-stealers are Giotto's luminous polyptych *Madonna and Child with Saints*, which takes pride of place in Room 3 as one of only three panel paintings in the world signed by the artist, and Raphael's *Santa Cecilia* (c.1515) in Room 15. This late altarpiece depicts the early Christian martyr and patron saint of music in ecstasy as she listens to a choir of angels in company of saints and Mary Magdalene. It was commissioned for a chapel dedicated to the saint in Bologna's Augustinian Church of San Giovanni in Monte; from the same church came Parmigianino's *Madonna and Child with Saints* (c.1530) now opposite the Raphael.

Not to be missed are the works by the great Bolognese baroque artists. Room 23 displays masterpieces by all three of the Carracci painters. The two brothers and their cousin worked collaboratively and their frescoes still adorn the greatest city palaces; but here the works by the individual artists highlight their differences in style as well as their similarities. Room 24 is dedicated to works by Guido Reni (1575–1642), including a portrait of his mother and the dramatic and skilful *Massacre of the Innocents*, distinguished by a bold use of colour and grace of line and form.

BOLOGNA AND THE BAROQUE

The members of the Bolognese school exerted one of the main influences on Baroque painting in Italy in the 17th century. Agostino (1557–1602), Annibale (1560–1609) and Ludovico Carracci (1555–1619), two brothers and a cousin, were leading figures in the movement against the affectations of Mannerism in Italian painting. Much in keeping with the desires of the Counter Reformation they revived the tradition of solidity and grandeur of the High Renaissance, stressing rigorous draftsmanship from life. Annibale's fame was such that he was called to Rome to decorate the Farnese gallery, considered in its time as a worthy successor to the frescoes of Michelangelo and Raphael. Guido Reni (1775–1642) was a pupil of the Carracci and was initially influenced by their classicising style. He left Bologna for Rome where he painted many of his finest works, but returned to his native city in 1613 to head a vast studio that exported religious works all over Europe.

In the 19th century the Bolognese painters fell from favour. The leading art critic, John Ruskin, described the school as having "no single virtue, no colour, no drawing, no character, no history, no thought". Their status suffered from Ruskin's attacks but the Carraccis and Guido Reni are now regarded among the greatest Italian painters of their age.

NORTH AND WEST OF CENTRE

From the maze of streets in the former Jewish ghetto to a cluster of medieval palaces and museums, this area of northern Bologna is packed with cultural attractions. When you have had your fill of sightseeing, the main streets of Via dell'Independenza, Via Ugo Bassi and Via Rizzoli provide plenty of retail distraction.

An alleyway in the ghetto

THE JEWISH GHETTO

Tucked into the triangle of Via Oberdan, Via Zamboni and Via Valdonica, in the shadow of the Due Torri, the former **ghetto** ㉕ is about mood rather than monuments. As a liberal, cosmopolitan city Bologna welcomed Jews who were booksellers and drapers, but in 1555, under papal rule, the ghetto was established. Unlike the crisply geometric street plan in 'Roman' Bologna this area is a warren of narrow alleys, predating the papal edict. Take Via de Giudei (Street of the Jews) to moody Via Canonica and **Via dell'Inferno** ㉖. The appropriately named 'Hell Street' became a virtual prison as only doctors were allowed to leave the ghetto at night. A plaque records the Holocaust but makes no reference to the expulsion of the Jews from here in 1593. The lofty buildings in Via Valdonica reflect the fact that the ghetto could only expand upwards. Recent gentrification has turned these tall tenements into desirable designer pads, so Hell Street is now a prestigious address – and one with a growing number of artisan workshops such as Calzoleria Max & Gio at No

22/A, creators of fine, made-to-measure shoes for men. The Palazzo Pannolini at 1/5 Via Valdonica is home to the **Museo Ebraico** (Jewish Museum; www.museoebraicobo.it; Sun–Thu 10am–6pm, Fri 10am–4pm) which aims to preserve, study and promote the cultural Jewish heritage of Bologna and the Emilia Romagna region. The history of the Jewish population is analysed through multi-media exhibits, documents and artefacts from former ghettos.

North of the ghetto, on Piazza San Martino is **San Martino** (daily 8am–noon and 4–7pm; free), a Carmelite church remodelled in the 14th century along Gothic lines. A quick visit reveals fragments of a Uccello battle scene and paintings by notable Bolognese artists, such as the Carracci. Also in this area look up to spot sealed arches and other vestiges of medieval churches, deconsecrated in Napoleon's day. But also expect signs for 'happy hour' and 'tattoos', proof that the university is nearby. Indeed, the square adjoins **Via Goito**, a popular place with students and a reminder that, for its size, Bologna has the greatest concentration of students in Italy.

The cathedral's lofty interior

CATTEDRALE METROPOLITANA DI SAN PIETRO

Via dell'Indipendenza was built to link the city centre and railway station in 1888.

At its southern end the main landmark is the **Cattedrale Metropolitana di San Pietro** ㉗ (daily 7.30am–6.45pm; free). Despite its nominal cathedral status and monumental interior, San Pietro plays second fiddle to the basilica of the city's patron saint, San Petronio. Architecturally and artistically it is certainly no match. In 1582 Pope Gregory XIII promoted the Bishop of Bologna to Archbishop and hence the cathedral rose to the rank of 'metropolitan church'. It was remodelled to be a showpiece of papal power and apart from a few relics in the Crypt and the red marble lions from the original portal there is little trace of the original Romanesque-Gothic structure. Stroll down Via Altabella to see the soaring **bell tower** which accommodates the *'la nonna'* (grandmother), the largest bell playable *'alla bolognese'*, a form of full circle ringing devised in the 16th century but which is sadly disappearing.

PALAZZO FAVA

Along **Via Manzoni**, west of Via dell'Indipendenza, the Fava palazzi are among the finest in the city. At No 2, the Palazzo Fava-Ghisilieri is now known simply as **Palazzo Fava** ㉘ (www.genusbononiae.it; Tue–Sun 10am–7pm; access may be limited when exhibitions are not showing). The palace was fully renovated as part of the Genus Bononiae project (see page 68) and reopened in 2011 as an exhibition centre. Blockbuster art shows are hosted here but it is also a treasure house of Carracci frescoes. In 1584 Filippo Fava commissioned Agostino, Annibale and Ludovico Carracci to decorate rooms on the *piano nobile* which gave rise to the first major fresco cycle of their career. This portrays the tragic tale of *Jason and Medea* and adorns the grand Sala di Giasone. Other halls of the palace were later decorated with scenes from Virgil's *Aeneid* by Ludovico and his pupils. On the ground floor of the palace two rooms display changing exhibits

Museo Civico Medievale courtyard

from the art collection of the Fondazione Cassa di Risparmio di Bologna.

MUSEO CIVICO MEDIEVALE

Next along is **Palazzo Ghisi-lardi Fava**, an archetypal Bolognese Gothic palace now home to the **Museo Civico Medievale ㉙** (Via Manzoni 4; www.museibologna.it/arte antica; Tue–Fri 9am–3pm, Sat–Sun 10am–6.30pm), a non-fusty medieval museum whose superbly arrayed medieval and Renaissance treasures illuminate the cultural and intellectual life of the city. A graceful, galleried courtyard leads to a series of elaborately sculpted sarcophagi depicting the greatest medieval scholars, and notably the lecturers in law. The collection's highlights are the coffered ceilings, stone statuary, gilded wood sculptures, and the monumental crosses that once adorned major city crossroads. Among many remarkable works are the *Pietra della Pace*, Stone of Peace by Corrado Fogolini, 1322, in Room 9, celebrating peace between the university and municipality following a period of conflict; the red marble tombstone of Bartolomeo da Vernazza (1348) in Room 11 and the statue of a *Madonna and Child* in polychrome terracotta by Jacopo della Quercia (1410) in Room 12. More specialist are the bronzes, weaponry, miniatures, medals and musical instruments. The vast and bizarre bronze statue of Pope Boniface VIII (1301) by Manno da Siena in Room 7 is a reminder of how the papacy liked to exert its power. Beyond the museum, at No 6, is the Casa Fava Conoscenti, one of the rare surviving tower houses, dating back to the 13th century.

SAN COLOMBANO

Just to the west in Via Parigi the deconsecrated Church complex of **San Colombano** ❸⓪ (www.genusbononiae.it; Tue–Sun 10am–7pm) makes a beautiful setting for the **Tagliavini Collection** of historical musical instruments. The late medieval church, decorated with faded frescoes, underwent major restoration before opening in 2010. Over 80 instruments are on display, among them spinets, harpsichords, clavichords and other keyboard instruments dating back five centuries and amassed by Bolognese musician and scholar, Luigi Ferdinando Tagliavini. Remarkably the instruments are all kept in perfect working order, played regularly and used for

A SUBTERRANEAN SERENISSIMA

It might not look like Venice but Bologna has an intricate network of over 60km (37 miles) of waterways, most of them running underground. From medieval times water was the source of economic progress and prosperity. The waters of the Savena, Reno and Aposa rivers were harnessed into canals both for domestic use and to provide energy for trades, particularly for the mills of the flourishing textile industry. Bologna became a leading silk producer in the 15th century and at the height of the industry had over 100 silk mills. The waterways were filled in during the 19th century but a port on the Navile Canal took goods and passengers down to the Po River and on to Venice, a system that served the city until the early 20th century. For a glimpse back into the era of waterways head for the Via Piella, just south of Piazza VIII Agosto, where the picturesque view over the Reno Canal from the little 'window' on the bridge gives a fleeting impression of Venice. For self-guided waterway-themed tours visit www.bolognawelcome.com, and for guided tours (in English and Italian) www.amicidelleacque.org.

Pick up a picnic

The covered Mercato delle Erbe at Via Ugo Bassi 25 (www.mercatodelleerbe.eu) is a great place for picnic supplies with its *salumerie* (for prosciutto and cheeses), bakers, *enotecas* and huge range of fresh fruit and veg. Alternatively there's a popular new food court with a range of freshly prepared, affordable dishes.

free monthly concerts from October to June. Among them are unique pieces such as an early 18th-century folding harpsichord and an earlier harpsichord with beautiful landscape decoration inside and out. The Oratory on the upper level displays a cycle of frescoes by the School of Carracci. Restoration works revealed the remains of a medieval crypt (accessible to the public) below the church, with a 13th-century mural *Crucifixion* attributed to Giunta Pisano and displayed behind glass.

Until Via dell'Indipendenza supplanted **Via Galliera** in 1888, this was the city's most majestic boulevard, built over a Roman road. The arcaded street is lined with noble palaces dating from the 15th to the 18th century. Here, as elsewhere, many of the terracotta-hued porticoes are built of recycled Roman and medieval bricks with decorative motifs in baked clay. The street runs north to the striking **Porta Galliera** (gateway), repeatedly destroyed and rebuilt five times between 1330 and 1511.

MAMBO

On the northwestern edge of the centre, transformed from a former municipal bakery which supplied bread to the Bolognesi during World War I, is **MAMbo** ㉛ (Museo d'Arte Moderna di Bologna, Bologna Modern Art Museum; Via Don Minzoni 14; www.mambo-bologna.org; Tue, Wed and Fri noon–6pm, Thur, Sat and Sun noon–8pm). The museum forms part of the new cultural **Manifattura delle Arti** complex, transformed from the old harbour and industrial area of the city.

MAMbo hosts temporary exhibitions and has a permanent collection tracing the history of Italian art from World War II to the present day. It is also temporary home to the **Museo Morandi** – transferred from Palazzo d'Accursio in the centre while its galleries are undergoing restoration. Georgio Morandi (1890–1964) was one of the great still-life painters of modern times. This collection spans his Cézanne-influenced early works, his moody landscapes and his enigmatic bottles and bowls. Some of his less-opaque works are landscapes of the Bolognese hills, where the artist withdrew in the face of Fascism. Morandi fans can also now visit the recently-restored house where Morandi lived and worked for most of his life, the **Casa Morandi** at 36 Via Fondazza, on the southeastern edge of the city (visits by

Bologna Museum of Modern Art (MAMbo)

The Fiera district

Northeast of centre the Bologna Exhibition Centre (www.bolognafiere.it) was built in 1961–75 beyond the ring road. It extends over 375,000 sq m (4,036,466 sq ft) and hosts on average 28 exhibitions a year. During the most popular shows hotels in Bologna are booked up months in advance.

appointment only, see www.mambo-bologna.org).

SAN FRANCESCO

Feeling far removed from the city bustle, to the west of the centre is the Gothic **San Francesco** 32 (daily 6.30am–noon and 3–7pm; free). Despite radical restoration and serious damage during Allied bombardments in 1943, the Franciscan church remains one of the most beautiful in the city. Completed in 1263 it is now admired for its rebuilt Gothic facade, ornate altarpiece and Renaissance tombs, including, in the left aisle, the tomb of Pope Alexander V who died in Bologna in 1410. The precious marble altarpiece depicting saints and naturalistic scenes from the life of St Francis was the work of the Venetian artists, Pier Paolo and Jacobello dalle Masegne (1393). Outside, on the street side of the church, are the four raised **Tombs of the Glossatori** (legal annotators) dating from the 13th century. Before the university had a fixed abode students attended lectures in monastic churches, including this one, where medicine and arts were taught. The university's presence lived on in the tombs of these illustrious doctors of law and medicine.

SOUTH OF THE CENTRE

The cultural highlight of this quarter, south of the centre, is San Domenico, a convent complex and treasure house of art. The winding Via Castiglione at its northern end is lined by imposing mansions from various eras including the fortress-like medieval Palazzo Pepoli, recently reinvented as a modern history museum. Many of the terracotta-hued palazzi afford glimpses of vaulted courtyards, sculpted gateways and richly frescoed interiors. West of San Domenico Via Marsili and Via d'Azeglio form part of the city's *passeggiata*, or ritual stroll, a chance to see the city at its most sociable.

The Piazza della Mercanzia south of the Due Torri feeds into the noble end of **Via Castiglione**. Both this street and Via Farini, an elegant shopping street, conceal waterways. The canal network linked to the River Po and the Adriatic generated the power for the silk and paper mills, brickworks and tanneries and for the millers, dyers and weavers who were the mainstay of the medieval economy. But when the district was gentrified in the 16th century, the nobility scorned these murky waters. Although finally covered in 1660, the canal still runs below Via Castiglione which explains why the pavements resemble canal banks.

Fiera district architecture

The austere medieval facade of the **Palazzo Pepoli Vecchio** at No 8 Via Castiglione belies a brand new interior, home to the **Museo della Storia di Bologna** ❸❸ (Museum of the History of Bologna; www.genusbon oniae.it; Tue, Wed, Fri, Sat, Sun 10am–7pm, Thu 10am– 10pm; ticket also valid for

Palazzo Fava Palazzo delle Esposizioni and San Colombano, Tagliavini Collection, see pages 61 and 63). The grandiose palace was built as the seat of the Pepoli, lords of Bologna in the mid-14th century, but was not completed until 1723. The interior underwent a total transformation in 2012 to become an innovative, interactive museum, dedicated to the historical and cultural heritage of Bologna. The tour spans 2,500 years of the city's distinguished history, focusing around the futuristic steel and glass Torre del Tempo (Tower of Time) which rises up from the courtyard. Through 3D films (and cartoons), mock-ups of Etruscan and Roman roads, photos and multimedia installations, the museum traces the evolution of the city from the Etruscans to the present day. The lively modern displays tend to attract more school groups and students than tourists and most of the labelling and videos are in Italian (though there are information sheets in English in most rooms).

GENUS BONONIAE, MUSEUMS IN THE CITY

The Museo della Storia di Bologna is one of the eight cultural attractions on the 'Genus Bononiae Museums in the City' itinerary (www.genusbononiae.it). The route takes in some of the city's most important churches and palaces that have been completely renovated for public use. Apart from one, all are within easy walking distance in the city centre. The attractions include the Palazzo Fava (see page 61) and the churches of San Colombano with the Tagliavini Collection (see page 63), Santa Maria della Vita (see page 41) and Santa Cristina, where concerts are held. Just out of town is San Michele in Bosco, a former monastery on a hill overlooking the city. The churches and palaces on the itinerary are managed, and some also owned by, the Fondazione Cassa di Risparmio di Bologna, a non-profit-making bank foundation.

BASILICA SAN DOMENICO

As you walk south along the Via Castiglione, the mood becomes subtly more domesticated. This was the key route to the Bolognese hills and access here was controlled by Porta Castiglione, one of ten surviving city gates. To the west the monumental **Basilica di San Domenico** 34 (Mon–Fri 9am–noon and 3.30–6pm, Sat 9am–noon and 3.30–5pm, Sun 3.30–5pm; charge for presbytery only) dominates

The Basilica di San Domenico, at the foot of the Bolognese hills

the cobbled **Piazza San Domenico**. The two mausoleums on the square, each with its tomb raised on pillars and protected by a canopy, celebrate renowned medieval law scholars Rolandino de' Passaggeri and Egidio Foscherari.

The Basilica was built to house the relics of San Domenico, founder of the Dominican order, who died here in 1221 when it was just the small church of San Nicolò of the Vineyards on the outskirts of Bologna. He was canonised in 1234 and his remains lie in an exquisite shrine within the church. The Dominican foundation was built in 1228–38 but was remodelled in baroque style. Although it has lost much of its late Romanesque and Renaissance purity it abounds in curious, canopied tombs and artworks by such luminaries as Michelangleo, Pisano and Filippino Lippi as well as by leading Bolognese artists. The **Cappella di San Domenico** (Chapel of St Dominic) holding the saint's tomb is half way down the basilica on the right. The spectacular

Piazza San Domenico, graced by a statue of the saint

Arca di San Domenico (Tomb of St Dominic) is the work of various leading artists, among them Niccolò da Bari – who acquired the name Niccolò dell'Arca following his highly acclaimed work on this tomb – Niccolò Pisano and Arnolfo di Cambio, both of the Pisan School. Niccolò da Bari died in 1492 and the Arca was completed by Michelangelo (a mere 19 years-old at the time) who carved two Bolognese saints, St Proculus and St Petronius holding a model of Bologna, and the angel on the right of the altar table holding up the candelabra. Above the Arca, Guido Reni's *St Dominic in Glory with Christ, the Madonna and Saints* decorates the dome, and hidden behind the shrine lies the precious reliquary of the head of St Dominic. Among the many other art works are the *Crucifix* (1250) by Giunta Pisano and the tomb of Taddeo Pepoli both in the left transept, the *Mystical Marriage of St Catherine* by Filippino Lippi in the small chapel beyond the right transept and the beautiful mid-16th-century marquetry choir stalls.

VIA D'AZEGLIO

In the late afternoon and early evening the pedestrianised **Via d'Azeglio ㉟**, west of San Domenico, is known as *il salotto*, or drawing room – the place for chatting over cocktails and designer shopping. It is a relaxed mix of happy families and glamorous Bologna *per bene* – the smart set. There are big-name boutiques here but the most sought-after shops are in neighbouring Galleria Cavour and Via Farini. The boldest of Bologna's senatorial palaces stands at No 31 – the 15th-century **Palazzo Bevilacqua** (No 31) in Tuscan style, with a rusticated sandstone facade, wrought iron balconies and a courtyard surrounded by a loggia. Here the Council of Trent met for two sessions in 1547 after fleeing an epidemic in Trent.

Tucked away in a corner west of Via d'Azeglio and off Via Collegio di Spagna lies a curious Spanish enclave. The crenellated **Collegio di Spagna** (visits only on request) was founded in 1365 by Cardinal Gil de Albornoz (representing the papacy) and bequeathed to Spanish scholars at Bologna University in 1365 as a glorified hostel. It continues to fulfil this function today, under the auspices of the Spanish Crown. Close by is the **Café de la Paix**, a café as peaceful as it sounds, with a special welcome for Spanish scholars. To the north east, on the corner of Via Val d'Aposa and Vicolo Spirito Santo, the **Spirito Santo** (no admission to the public) is an exquisite jewel-box of a church. Under the medieval

Lucio Dalla

If you happen to be in Via d'Azeglio at 6pm, you will hear the music of Lucio Dalla (1943–2012), the much-loved Bolognese singer-songwriter (his *Caruso* sung by Pavarotti sold nine million copies).
The music is streamed from Via d'Azeglia 15, where Dalla lived. His funeral was held in the Basilica of San Petronio and over 50,000 people came to the Piazza to bid him farewell.

streets here runs a secret river, the d'Aposa.

THE BOLOGNA HILLS

San Michele in Bosco

Crowning a hilltop to the southwest of the city and linked to it by the world's longest portico is the famous **Santuario della Madonna di San Luca** ③⑥ (daily 7am–12.30pm and 2.30–7pm, Nov–Feb until 5pm). Dating from 1732 the conspicuous pink basilica took 50 years to build, is 3.8km (2.3 miles) long, has 666 arches and winds its way up from Piazza di Porta Saragozza. You are rewarded at the top with fine views of the Apennines. (If you don't fancy the whole hike take bus No 20 to the Arco Meloncello and walk from there or take the little tourist train from the centre in season.) The 18th-century sanctuary is richly decorated and houses a much-revered Byzantine-style image of the Madonna, probably dating from medieval times but once believed to have been painted by St Luke. Every Ascension Week she is taken down the hill to the Cathedral of San Pietro, with crowds lining the Via Saragozza to see the procession go by. The church brings barefoot pilgrims and other worshippers as well as joggers and cyclists who go up the hill to work off the pasta.

Lording it over Bologna to its south is **San Michele in Bosco** ③⑦ (daily 9am–noon and 4–7pm; free; 30 mins on foot or take No 30 bus), a religious complex with an annexed monastery that has served as an orthopaedic hospital since 1880. The Fondazione Cassa di Risparmio di Bologna now manages the vast area, including the octagonal cloister and library, and the church complex features on the Genus Bononiae museum itinerary (see page 68). The sweeping views, which were admired by Stendhal when he passed through Bologna in 1817, embrace the entire city.

EXCURSIONS FROM BOLOGNA

With excellent rail links Bologna makes a good base for excursions to the handsome historic cities of Emilia-Romagna. (It is only around half an hour to Modena and Ferrara, an hour to Parma, 80 mins to Ravenna, 60–90 mins to Rimini). Apart from culture, the region is a gourmet's delight and many visitors come on gastronomic tours taking in artisan producers of Parma ham, Mortadella, traditional balsamic vinegar of Modena, Parmigiano Reggiano – as well as local wine producers. The Langhirano valley is home to around 500 authorised

You'll never go hungry in Bologna

producers of the famous *prosciutto crudo* di Parma, many open to the public for tastings and purchases. On plains north of Parma there are Parmesan cheese-making cooperatives and around Modena balsamic vinegar distilleries where the vinegar is aged in wooden barrels for up to 25 years.

PARMA

Parma ❸❽ is a byword for fine living, from Parmesan and Parma ham to music and Mannerist art. At the heart of the city a network of quiet old streets opens on to the harmonious **Piazza Duomo** where the Lombard Romanesque **Cathedral** (www.cattedralediparma.it; daily 9am–12.30pm and 3–7pm; free) and the graceful rose marble Baptistery form a fine ensemble. Inside the cathedral, decorating the central dome in a triumph of *trompe-l'œil,* is Corregio's great masterpiece: the *Assumption of the Virgin (1526–30).* This boldly illusionistic work, Corregio's last fresco, paved the way for Baroque art but found little favour with the church. The neighbouring **Baptistery** (daily 9am–12.30pm and 3–6.30pm) is a jewel of the Italian Romanesque – a beautiful octagonal building with elaborately carved reliefs on the exterior and portals by sculptor and architect, Benedetto Antelami (1150–1230). The interior is an illuminated manuscript awash with vividly coloured 13th-century biblical scenes, influenced by Byzantine art. Antelami and his assistants created the series of sculptures, showing the seasons, the signs of the zodiac and the labours

Frogs' legs fresco

A canon of Parma's cathedral criticised Corregio's fresco of the *Assumption of the Virgin* as 'a stew of frogs' legs', but Titian, recognising the artist's triumph of illusionism, decreed that if the dome were turned upside down and filled with gold it would not be as valuable as Correggio's frescoes.

of the month. The masterly Antelami is also believed to have been the architect of the Baptistery.

Behind the cathedral the 16th-century Renaissance church of **San Giovanni Evangelista** (www.monas terosangiovanni.com; Mon-Sat 8.30am–11.45am and 3–5.30pm, Sun 3–5.30pm) with a Baroque facade also has a cupola decorated with a fine Correggio fresco: *The Vision of St John on Patmos*, depicting Christ descending to John. Northwest of Piazza del Duomo, in a former Benedictine convent, the

Al fresco dining in Parma

Camera di San Paolo (Tue–Fri 8.30am–2pm, Sat 8.30am–6pm, Sat in Jul and Aug 8.30am–2pm) was one of the private rooms in the apartments of the unconventional and learned Abbess of San Paolo, called Giovanna da Piacenza. In 1519 she commissioned Correggio to decorate the room with a feast for the senses, including mischievous *putti* and a view of Chastity as symbolised by the goddess Diana. It was Correggio's first large-scale commission in Parma.

The **Palazzo della Pilotta** on Piazzale della Pace is the city's cultural heart and home to the **Galleria Nazionale** (Tue–Sat 8.30am–7pm, Sun 8.30am–2pm) with works by locals such as Correggio and Il Parmigianino, along with Venetian, Tuscan and other Emilian artists. The palazzo also houses the archaeological museum, housing pre-Roman and Roman artefacts, the Palatine Library and the **Teatro Farnese**, an imposing wooden theatre with a revolving stage, based on Palladio's masterpiece, the Teatro Olimpico at Vicenza. It is still used for theatrical performances.

MODENA

Modena 39 is the home of Pavarotti, Maserati and Ferrari, and its wonderfully preserved historic centre is Unesco-listed. Yet it is rarely visited by tourists. The success of the food, sleek Ferrari cars and ceramics industries has been instrumental in making tourism a mere after-thought in this cosseted land of plenty. A morning's sightseeing in the historic centre could be followed by a meal at an *osteria* ranking No 2 in the World's 50 Best Restaurants (see page 114 and reserve well in advance), then perhaps a visit to a traditional balsamic vinegar distill-ery, **Acetaia di Giorgio** (Via Cabassi 67; www.acetaiadigiorgio.

Modena's Piazza Grande, dominated by the Romanesque Duomo

it) to learn the tricks of the trade and taste the unctuous Aceto Balsamico Tradizionale di Modena vinegar.

Modena's city centre is dominated by the **Duomo** (daily 7am–12.30pm and 3.30–7pm) one of the masterpieces of the Italian Romanesque for both its architecture and sculpture. The grandiose marble cathedral and adjoining bell tower are Unesco World Heritage Sites. In a tribute, rare for the 12th century, the names of both the architect, Lanfranco, and the master sculptor, Wiligelmo da Modena, are recorded on inscriptions on the facade. Countess Matilda of Tuscany, ruler of Modena, commissioned Lanfranco, the greatest architect of the time, to mastermind the cathedral which would house the remains of St Geminiano, patron saint of the city. Wiglielmo equalled him in creating the exuberant friezes of griffins and dragons, peacocks and trailing vine leaves. On the southern side, the main portal is flanked by stylised Roman-style lions; over the doorway on the left is Wiglielmo's finest work, the depiction of the *Creation and Fall of Adam and Eve*. On the northern side the sculptured Porta della Pescheria is decorated with the cycle of the months. The softly lit interior reveals brick-vaulted naves and such treasures as the rood-screen, a Romanesque masterpiece, as well as the crypt sculpted by Wiglielmo. Alongside the apse rises the leaning **Torre della Ghirlandina**, the octagonal 12th-century bell tower built with slabs of marble recycled from Roman ruins.

To the northwest of the cathedral, on Piazza Sant'Agostino, stands the **Palazzo dei Musei** (www.museicivici.modena. it) where the d'Este court amassed Modena's finest art collection and library and now hosting the city's museums and art galleries. The most interesting are the **Galleria Estense** (www.galleriaestense.org; Mon 8.30am–2pm, Tue–Sat 8.30am–7pm, Sun 2–7pm), a rich collection of works by Emilian, Flemish and Venetian artists, and the **Biblioteca**

Pavarotti's house

The House and Museum of Luciano Pavarotti, 8km (5 miles) from the centre of Modena (www.casamuseo lucianopavarotti.it) gives a glimpse into the life of the late maestro. Opened in 2015, it displays personal memorabilia and recordings of great performances.

Estense which displays rare manuscripts, seals and maps, as well as the priceless Bibbio Borso, the beautifully illustrated bible of Borso d'Este, first Duke of Modena. On Piazza Roma, northeast of the cathedral, the austere and immense **Palazzo Ducale** (Ducal Palace) was the former court of the d'Este dynasty. It is now Italy's top military academy, with no access for the public, but the ducal park behind has been converted into public and botanical gardens.

FERRARI MUSEUMS

Ferrari, Maserati and Lamborghini sports cars are all produced in Modena so a passion for speed goes with the territory. Enzo Ferrari founded his firm in 1939 and the company is still producing cars in the Maranello factories in the industrial outskirts. Modena now has its own Ferrari museum: the **Museo Enzo Ferrari** (www.museomodena.ferrari.com) where Ferraris and Maseratis are displayed in a gigantic showroom and Enzo Ferrari's fascinating life story is related in the converted workshop of his father. A regular shuttle bus connects the museum with Maranello (20km/12.5 miles from Modena) where the **Museo Ferrari** (www.museomaranello. ferrari.com) showcases the world's largest collection of Ferraris, with models through the ages – and a simulator where visitors can experience driving a Ferrari single-seater on the Monza track. Every Ferrari victory in the Grand Prix is celebrated by the priest ringing the bells of the Maranello parish church – which gives you some idea of the fanaticism of the locals.

FERRARA

Beguiling **Ferrara** was a stronghold of the high-living dukes of Este – archetypically scheming, murderous, lovable Renaissance villains who ruled from 1200–1600 and from Ferrara-controlled territory embracing Parma, Modena and Garfagnana in Tuscany. During its Renaissance heyday, the dynasty drew artists of the stature of Piero della Francesca and Mantegna, turning the Ferrara court into a 'princely gar-den of delights'. From the 17th to the 19th century travellers found Ferrara something of a ghost town with few inhabitants and grass growing in the streets. However since its bombing in World War II the city has revived and in 1995 was declared a Unesco World Heritage Site.

The gleaming Museum Enzo Ferrari in Modena

The heart of the town is still dominated by the formidable **Castello Estense** (www.castelloestense.it; Sep–May 9.30am–5.30pm, Jun–Aug 9.30am–1.30pm and 3–7pm, closed Mon in Jan, Jul, Aug, Oct, Nov and Dec), a 14th-century moated fortress where guides tell delightfully dubious tales of what went on in the dungeons. As the d'Este dynasty's seat the medieval fortress was gradually transformed into a gracious Renaissance palace but retains elements from both incarnations. Most of the artistic treasures were spirited away to Modena when Ferrara's rival became the Ducal capital in 1598, and the great works of the Ferrarese school are dispersed in European public collections, notably the National Gallery in London. However the noble apartments retain some outstanding frescoed ceilings. To sample noble dishes dating back to the d'Este court, head for the **Hostaria Savonarola** in Piazza Savonarola, adjoining Castle Square. Try a plate of *tortelli di ricotta* or *cappellaci di zucca*, pumpkin-filled pasta parcels.

South of the Castello Estense is the triple-gabled Romanesque and Gothic **Cathedral** (Mon–Sat 7.30am–noon and 3.30–6.30pm, Sun 7.30am–12.30pm and 3.30–7pm; free). The facade has rich sculptural detail: from the lunette of *St George Killing the Dragon* to the loggia and the baldachin adorned with sculptures of the Madonna and Child. The disappointing baroque interior is redeemed by a Byzantine baptismal font and the museum, which holds sculptures by Jacopo

On your bike

Ferrara is Italy's most bike-friendly city – there are 2.1 bikes per inhabitant. For bike-hire, cycling suggestions in the traffic-free centre and cycling tourism in the province (including the popular 100km/62.5 mile route that runs along the River Po towards the sea) visit www.ferraraterraeacqua.it.

della Quercia and two masterpieces by Cosmè Tura decorating organ shutters and representing *The Annunciation* and *St George and the Princess*. The **Piazza della Cattedrale** is best appreciated from the café terrace of the Pasticceria Leon d'Oro. The piazza comes alive during the Palio in May, a medieval tournament dating back to 1259, and the Buskers' Festival in August, which is biggest of its kind in the world.

The delightful Castello Estense in Ferrara

Almost every vermillion brick palazzo in Ferrara has a link to the powerful dynasty. You can get a sense of their grandeur among the Renaissance palazzi of the Corso Ercole I d'Este, part of an ambitious 15th-century urban expansion, Addizione Erculea. The d'Estes' **Palazzo dei Diamanti** (Tue, Wed, Fri–Sun 9am–2pm, Thu 9am–7pm) takes its name from the 8,500 diamond-shaped marble stones on its facade. The palace stages prestigious modern-art exhibitions and is also home to the **Pinacoteca Nazionale** (Tue, Wed, Fri–Sun 9am–2pm, Thu 9am–7pm), which displays frescoes from several ruined churches and School of Ferrara paintings by Cosmè Tura and Francesco del Cossa.

The main thoroughfare, **Corso Giovecca**, has a sweep of patrician palaces designed to link the medieval core with the Renaissance city. The most regal residence is **Palazzina di**

Ravenna, one-time capital of the Western World

Marfisa d'Este (Tue–Sun 9.30am–1pm and 3–6pm) which was a *delizia*, a Renaissance pleasure palace dedicated to satisfying every whim. The noble apartments feature Renaissance furniture, a portrait gallery and ceilings studded with grotesque motifs. The frescoed loggia, which is used for concerts, is a lingering terrace of the sumptuous rural retreat that this once was.

On the south-eastern edge of the city the 14th-century **Palazzo Schifanoia** (Tue–Sat 9.30am–6pm) was the summer residence of Borso d'Este, Duke of Ferrara. The name translates as 'Palace for Banishing Boredom', a reflection of its role as the d'Este court's first and finest pleasure palace. The austere facade was once as richly frescoed as the interior. A highlight of the palace-museum is the restored **Salone dei Mesi** (Room of the Months) on the first floor which is decorated with a delightful cycle of frescoes depicting the four seasons. Here allegorical tales are interwoven with everyday scenes of the court.

RAVENNA

With its air of quiet prosperity, **Ravenna** ❹ seems like a provincial sleepy town that just happens to contain the finest mosaics in Europe. It has no less than eight Unesco World Heritage Sites in the shape of Byzantine mosaics. Like Venice, Ravenna was built on a series of islands in a lagoon. It thrived as a Roman city, was the last enclave of the Roman Empire in the West and even shone throughout the so-called Dark Ages. In the 5th and 6th centuries, Roman and Byzantine cultures converged in Ravenna and bequeathed the city superb mosaics, transforming it into a luminous Western Byzantium. Since the early mosaics were designed by Greek artists from Constantinople, the inspiration was as much from pagan temples as Christian churches.

In the northern corner of the city centre is the three-storey brick **Basilica of San Vitale** (daily Apr–Oct 9am–7pm, Nov–Mar 9am–5pm; ticket includes entry to Basilica of Sant'Apollinare Nuovo, Neoniano Baptistery, Mausoleum of Galla Placidia and Archiepiscopal Museum and Chapel and the opening times are the same). This simple octagonal-plan brick church, consecrated in the 6th century, has an interior decorated with superb mosaics, remarkable for their clarity of design and colour and their intricate detail. In the same grounds is the oldest of the Byzantine monuments, the 5th-century **Mausoleum of Galla Placidia**, named after the Christian half-sister of Honorius, the Roman emperor who transferred the capital to Ravenna in AD 402. She ruled in the emperor's absence, and later married a Visigoth king and a Roman emperor before returning to Ravenna. This tiny Latin cross-shaped mausoleum has a plain brick exterior but inside a stunning tapestry of mosaics – the oldest in Ravenna. The mystical atmosphere is intensified by the strikingly simple style of the mosaics, including the cobalt-blue sky sprinkled with gold stars.

East of the city centre, the **Basilica di Sant'Apollinare Nuovo** was built by the Christian Ostrogoth King Theodoric in the 6th century using Greek marbled columns recycled from a pagan temple. The mosaic-encrusted interior is studded with scenes recalling life in Ravenna and biblical anecdotes. On the left, the mosaics depict 22 virgins leaving the ancient port of Classe to follow the Three Magi; opposite the solemn procession of 26 martyrs is wonderfully naturalistic, despite a traditional format. Although created in different periods the mosaics present great unity, infusing Byzantine decorative genius with the awe and mystery of Catholicism. These elements come together in a sublime *Christ in Majesty*.

Some 5km (3 miles) south of the centre stands the Byzantine **Basilica di Sant'Apollinare in Classe** (open daily 8.30am–7.30pm). If this sumptuous basilica seems marooned in the countryside, it is symbolic of the abandonment of the site after the silting up of Classe, Rome's largest Adriatic port. The focus of attention is the apse and choir with breath-taking mosaics, full of lovely landscape details. The presence of the docile lambs in the pastoral scene of the Good Shepherd leading his flock is a reminder that Ravenna was a beacon of artistic excellence at a time when sheep were grazing on the Roman forum. The lustrous tints and textures led Dante, who had sought refuge in Ravenna, to describe the mosaics as having 'the sweet colour of oriental sapphires'.

Ponte di Tiberio, Rimini

Rimini beach is lined with resorts

RIMINI

A long sandy beach, lively hotels and nightclubs make **Rimini** ❷ a favourite playground for sun-seekers. But inland, on the other side of the railway, it has a quiet historic centre which retains Roman and Renaissance monuments. The most prized monument is the unfinished 15th-century **Tempio Malatestiano** (Mon–Fri 8.30am–noon and 3.30–6.30pm, Sat 8.30am–12.30pm and 3.30–7pm, Sun 9am–12.30pm and 3.30–6.30pm; free), a Renaissance design of the famous Florentine architect and art theorist Leon Battista Alberti, who was inspired by the wealth of Roman architecture remaining in the city. More pagan temple than church, it served as a mausoleum for the cultivated but cruel tyrant Sigismondo Malatesta and his wife Isotta degli Atti. Now the city cathedral, the Tempio showcases a crucifix attributed to Giotto, as well as Piero della Francesca's fresco of *Sigismondo Malatesta Kneeling before his Patron Saint Sigismondo* (1451) and the sculpted Malatesta tombs – works far finer than the debauched rulers deserved.

WHAT TO DO

ENTERTAINMENT

Bologna is lively all year round, but particularly from March to June and September to December when the cultural season is in full swing. The huge student population ensures that the city has a vibrant nightlife scene – during term-time at least; and during the long summer holiday, when the students abandon the city, the authorities stage a season of music and cinema to content its visitors. Bologna stages great music, both classical and contemporary, and is the only Italian city to have been appointed a Unesco Creative City of Music (2006). The tourist office website (www.bolognawelcome.com) is a good source of information for the host of cultural events and the venues for nightlife.

CLASSICAL MUSIC, OPERA AND THEATRE

The **Teatro Comunale** (Largo Respighi 1; www.tcbo.it) is the main venue for the performing arts, from opera and ballet to orchestral and chamber music. Tickets are available from the box office, the Bologna Welcome tourist office in Piazza Maggiore or online. Concerts are also organised in other city theatres, churches and at the **Conservatorio G.B. Martini** (Piazza Rossini 2; www.consbo.it), a concert hall within a former Augustine convent. Many churches, such as Santo Stefano, San Domenico, Santa Maria dei Servi and Santa Cristina, double up as concert venues. The frescoed **Museo Internazionale e Biblioteca della Musica** (Strada Maggiore 34, www.museibologna.it) is both an exceptional museum of music and a venue for classical concerts and events; likewise the restored church of **San Colombano** is home to the Tagliavini collection of historical musical instruments and

Designer shops line the elegant Portico del Pavaglione

hosts free monthly classical concerts from October to June. The central **Auditorium Teatro Manzoni** (Via De'Monari 1/2; www.auditoriumanzoni.it), set within a finely restored art nouveau palazzo, hosts a range of concerts from classical to jazz, rock and contemporary. The **Teatro Europa** (Piazza Costituzione 4; www.teatroeuropa.it) is a multi-purpose venue for ballet, musicals and drama located near the Fiera exhibition centre.

CINEMA

The **Cineteca di Bologna** (www.cinetecadibologna.it) is located within the transformed Manifattura Tabacchi, a former tobacco factory on the northwest edge of the city, and now a major cultural centre. The Cineteca's state-of-the-art Cinéma Lumière (with the Sala Scorsese and Sala Mastroianni)

Sotto le stelle del Cinema, a popular open-air film festival held in Piazza Maggiore in July

honours the history of the moving image, screening restored classics, retrospectives and rare films always in the original version. The Cineteca also hosts Bologna's film festivals. Within the same complex is the Renzo Renzi Library, dedicated to the conservation and study of film and photography and the archives of Charlie Chaplin and Pier Paolo Pasolini (viewing by appointment only). The **Capitol** cinema (www.capitolmultisala.com) near the station shows blockbusters in their original version, with Italian subtitles.

NIGHTLIFE

As a lively university city, Bologna has no shortage of bars, pubs, clubs, live jazz and late-opening restaurants. The early evening involves the ritual *passeggiata*, the people-watching parade, partly viewed from a succession of café terraces. In summer Bologna's parks are transformed into party venues, with the atmosphere resembling a less boisterous version of a German *Biergarten*. The most popular spot is **La Montagnola Park** which has live jazz and rock music, as well as stalls selling beer, wine and fast food. Open-air concerts, films and festivities are also staged in city squares, such as Piazza Maggiore; other events take place in streets, museums and under the porticoes.

In general the liveliest area in town is the **Via Zamboni** in the university district which has the greatest concentration of late-night music haunts. The **Via del Pratello** area on the west side of the city also appeals to night-owls with pubs and bars (frequently serving food as well as drinks) interspersed with music clubs and inns. The nightlife is predominantly student-orientated although there are bar-restaurants that appeal to all ages. A good example is **Cantina Bentivoglio** (www.cantinabentivoglio.it) where the best jazz in Bologna can be enjoyed in palatial 16th-century cellars. An equally ageless, classless place is **Osteria de' Poeti** (www.osteriade poeti.com) where, along with a friendly owner, brick-vaulted ceilings, 16th-century stonework and picturesque wine barrels provide a mellow mood for live jazz and folk music. Jazz has been thriving since the arrival of American troops at the end of World War II and can be heard in many other *osterie* throughout the city.

SHOPPING

Bologna's best buys are food and wine, fashion and designer goods. Shopping here is anything but provincial, and ranges from one-off boutiques to top designer brands – many of which started out in the city or in the wider region. Bologna's up-market fashion outlets are all central, and clustered around the Piazza Maggiore area, some in beautifully restored palazzi. The pedestrianised Via d'Azeglio is a lovely place to shop, as is Via dell'Archiginnasio, the porticoed area behind San Petronio known as the Pavaglione. The smartest boutiques line Via Farini and the discreet shopping galleries

APERITIVO TIME

Cocktails are part of Bolognese nightlife and Happy Hour is a moveable feast, from 6–9.30pm. The price of a drink may seem steep, but *stuzzichini* (appetizers) and often a whole buffet may be included and can provide a meal in itself. A favourite cocktail is an Aperol Spritz, made with orange liqueur, prosecco and a splash of soda. Among the popular cocktail spots are: Zanarini behind the Basilica, rendez-vous of well-heeled Bolognesi; Eataly, the popular 'marketplace' Italian chain at Via degli Orefici; and Ex Forno, the trendy café at the Bologna Museum of Modern Art. But the most unusual spot has to be the atmospheric Le Stanze (see page 112) housed within a Bentivoglio chapel.

nearby. Galleria Cavour, a luxurious arcade linking Via Farini with Via de'Foscherari, is the place to go for the big designer brands. More mainstream shopping, from high fashion to footwear, can be found along Via dell'Indipendenza, Via Rizzoli and Via Ugo Bassi, the high streets of Bologna. Coin, at Via Rizzoli 7, part of the chain department store, is worth checking out for affordable clothes made in Italy.

Giorgio Armani was born in nearby Piacenza

GASTRONOMY

Bologna has a dazzling array of gastronomic delicacies. Moreover, Emilia Romagna, as a region, is dedicated to preserving its unique branded produce, from Parmesan cheese and Parma ham to balsamic vinegar, extra-virgin olive oil and wine. All of these can be picked up in delicatessens, markets, or sampled directly from the producers. The Bolognesi attach great importance to finding the right foodstuffs and you are likely to find good quality just about everywhere, even in the simplest street market.

The Bologna Welcome office (www.bolognawelcome.com) has information on gastronomic tours where you can track down tasty cheeses, cured meats, truffles, dried mushrooms and genuine balsamic vinegar – just to name a few. In central Bologna, just off Piazza Maggiore, the warren of alleys making up the **Mercato di Mezzo** is a feast for the eyes with its specialised food shops, stalls piled high with fresh fruit, fish

Food shopping is an art in Bologna

and cheese and a covered market which sells the finest regional produce. Along Via Pescherie Vecchie, Via degli Orefici and Via Drapperie shopkeepers tempt passers-by with slices of *mortadella* and *prosciutto*. **Tamburini** (Via Caprarie 1; www.tamburini.com) is the city's most endearing delicatessen, brimming with Bolognese and Emilian specialities. Try them out at their VeloCibò self-service. For homemade pasta and bread look no further than **Paolo Atti & Figli** (Via Caprarie 7; www.paoloatti.com), a Bolognese institution dating back to 1900 and still in the same family. Pastas are all made on the spot and their beautifully wrapped and boxed creations make perfect Italian gifts to take back home. Also in the heart of the market is **Salumeria Simoni** (Via Drapperie 5/2a; www.salumeriasimoni.it) which is stacked to the brim with hams and cheeses. A step inside the shop may well tempt you to sign up for one of their gastronomy tours or at least to try out the delicacies with local wine.

Chocoholics should head for **Majani** (Via Carbonesi 5; www.majani.it), one of Italy's oldest chocolate shops whose delicacies were one-time favourites with European royalty. Displays are laid out in a splendid art-nouveau shop-front and art-deco interior. Try the Fiat Majani, created for the launch of the new Fiat Tipo 4, hence the four layers of velvety chocolate. Another irresistible *chocolatier* is **Roccati** (Via Clavature 17; www.roccaticioccolato.com) where you can watch the chocolate creations being sculpted in the workshop. Their speciality is *gianduja*, chocolate with hazelnut. For divine patisserie head for **Regina di Quadri** on Via Castiglione (www.reginadiquadri. eu), with its show-stopping cakes and pastries.

Modena is renowned for *aceto balsamico* (balsamic vinegar) but the factory-produced variety made of wine vinegar bears scant resemblance to the traditional product – a subtle, unctuous substance that can only be sold after ageing in wooden casks for at least 12 years (red label), 18 years (silver label) or 25 years (gold label). Look for *Aceto Balsamico Tradizionale di Modena* or *di Reggio Emilia*. The real thing is a reduction of pressed and cooked Trebbiano and Lambrusco grapes, with a complex sweet and sour flavour, a hint of wood, and a high price

PASTA PERFECT

What better souvenir than to be able to recreate perfect hand-made pasta back home? Bologna has over 20 cookery schools, which is perhaps not surprising in what is generally regarded as the culinary capital of Italy. A half-day course might take in a tour of the local market with its fresh produce and gourmet delis (with tastings on the way) and a lesson on how to make an authentic *ragù alla bolognese* (bolognese sauce) and prepare the egg pasta from scratch. After all the hard work you can sit back and enjoy the fruits of your labour – along with a glass or two of good *vino*. The hands-on lessons are adapted to level of experience and culinary requirements; they are usually held in very small groups and last a couple of hours, a half or whole day or longer. A few days' notice may be required, though last-minute requests are always worth trying. Costs vary considerably from €90–160 for a half-day class (followed by lunch, which is included in the price). Full details are available from the Bologna Welcome tourist office (www.bolognawelcome.com).

tag. Expect to pay €40–80 for a small bottle, but whether you are using it on Parmigiano Reggiano and *mortadella* or drizzling it over strawberries or *gelato*, all you will need is a few drops. Bottles can be bought from *acetaiae* (balsamic vinegar producers) in the region or from high-end food shops in Bologna.

There are several excellent *enoteche* (specialised wine stores) where you can try and buy local wines, among them **Enoteca Italiana** (Via Marsala 2/6) with a wonderful selection of Italian and particularly Emilia Romagna wines. It is run by two award-winning sommeliers who will guide you round – and suggest wines to go with regional treats such as Parma ham and Mortadella which are served here all day.

MARKETS

The city markets are full of character, atmosphere and delicious foodstuffs, ideal for picnics or as presents to take home. In the centre are the **Mercato di Mezzo** and adjoining open-air food market as well as the renovated **Mercato delle Erbe** at Via Ugo Bassi 25, a large and lively covered market with wonderful local produce and a new food court where you can sit and make the most of prepared market produce. The **Mercato Antiquario**, occupying Piazza Santo Stefano and the streets nearby, is an antiques and curios market, with vintage clothing and jewellery, held on the second Saturday and Sunday of the month from 8.30am–6pm (7pm in summer, closed Jul and Aug). Another antiquarian fixture is the **Mercato dell'Antiquariato** on Via Matteotti on the first

Nun selling local produce

Tuesday of the month and from Mar–Jun and Sep–Dec also the second Tuesday of the month. The **DecoMela Art and San Giuseppe Colours** on Via San Giuseppe, which take place on alternative weekends (Fri–Sun except Jan, Jul and Aug), are handicraft-collectors' haunts, with pottery, lamps, fabrics and semi-precious stones. **La Piazzola** market occupies the Piazza VIII Agosto every Friday and Saturday and is worth checking out for bargain shoes and clothes, including vintage; it also sells leather, bric-à-brac, arts and crafts.

Markets and food stalls abound with locally grown fruit and vegetables

SPORT

Basketball (*pallacanestro*) in Bologna is hugely popular and the city's Virtus team (www.virtus.it) is one of the best in Europe. Tickets are available at www.ticketone.it or at the Unipol Arena in Casalecchio di Reno, southwest of the city, where they play. Their home rivals are Fortitudo (in the 2nd Division) who play at PalaDozza (or 'the Palazzo'), a multipurpose arena with a capacity of 5,570 in Piazza Azzarita, northwest of the centre. As elsewhere in Italy **football** (soccer) is a passion. Bologna FC (Football Club, www.bolognafc.it) in the First Division has won the Italian league championship seven times, and when they are playing at home thousands of fans will be heading to the Renato dall'Ara stadium,

Fabulous cars at the Museo Ferruccio Lamborghini

Via Andrea Costa 174, about 3km (2 miles) west of the city centre. Tickets can be bought at various tobacconists or online at www.listicket.com.

MOTOR VALLEY

In the heart of Emilia's 'Land of Motors', with its Ferrari and Lamborghini-inspired museums, Bologna is a motor-lover's dream. The museums can be visited independently by public transport or on a guided tour – details of which can be found at the Bologna Welcome tourist office and on their website (www.bolognawelcome.com). For the Ferrari Museums in Maranello and Modena see page 78. The **Museo Ferruccio Lamborghini** (www.museolamborghini.com) moved in 2013 from Dosso near Ferrara to Argelato, 15km (9 miles) north of Bologna. Visitors who book ahead can tour the company factory with Fabio Lamborghini, a nephew of the famous founder Ferruccio. For motorbike fans the **Ducati Museum** at the Ducati Factory (www.ducati.com), 9km (5.5 miles) northwest of the city centre, displays the models that have made the brand famous worldwide.

ACTIVE PURSUITS

Few of the central hotels have fitness centres but to get rid of excess tortellini you could climb the Asinelli Tower (498 steps), stretch your legs in the Parco della Montagnola or Giardini Margherita or walk 6km (4 miles) up to the hilltop sanctuary of San Luca.

The city is well equipped with public swimming pools including the **Piscina Sterlino** (Via A. Murri 113) southeast of the city, with one olympic-sized pool, two 25m ones and a green area with bar, parasols and sunbeds in summer, and the **Carmen Longo-Stadio** at Bologna's football stadium centre (Via dello Sport, www.sogese.com), with indoor and outdoor pools. The **Circolo Tennis Bologna** (Viale Rino Cristiani 2; www.circolotennisbologna.com) in the Margherita Gardens has seven courts, floodlit from April to September and covered for the rest of the year. It also has a 25m swimming pool and a gym. For relaxation and wellbeing, the **Mare Terme San Petronio** (Via Irnerio 12/A; www.maretermalebolognese. it), near Parco della Montagnola, offers thermal spa waters, sauna, pool, hot tubs and beauty treatments. For those who prefer a Turkish bath the **Hammam Bleu** (Vicolo Barbazzi 4; www.hammam.it), centrally located just south of the Basilica of San Petronio, has treatments ranging from basic (€55) to the full works (€185). Booking is essential, as is a membership fee of €10 per person.

SPORTS IN EMILIA ROMAGNA

Emilia Romagna can compete with the sportiest of regions, with activities ranging from sailing to cycling, riding to alpine skiing, ice-skating to Formula One racing. The landscape lends itself to a wealth of possibilities: the lofty Apennines become small-scale ski slopes in winter but revert to rugged open-walking country in spring and summer. The flat area around Ferrara is gentle cycling country with inviting tracks created on the raised canal banks in the Po Delta area. The Ferrara tourist authorities have set up superb cycling routes, with guides, to get you effortlessly around the Po Delta. The region is well endowed with 'bike hotels' – places offering a full service from picnic hampers to bike repairs and maps for the next stretch of route.

CHILDREN'S BOLOGNA

Bologna is not the obvious choice for children, especially given the sparsity of parks and gardens in the centre. Active young-sters might enjoy the challenge of 498 steps up the **Torre degli Asinelli**, older ones will no doubt be fascinated by the **Teatro Anatomico** where human dissections took place, the **Specola** (Observatory) and **waxwork museums** of the University (see page 54). The innovative **Museum of History at Palazzo Pepoli** is geared to all ages with 3-D films and reconstructions, and the **Sala Borsa multimedia centre**, right in the centre, is a good place to chill out with computers or watching films.

Ice cream is always a winner

Take sports fans to see Virtus play **basketball** and to let off steam **climb** (or jog/bike up) the world's longest portico to the Sanctuary of the Madonna di San Luca. The best park for picnics (or snacks at the Chalet dei Giardini Margherita on the bridge over the central lake) is the **Giardini di Margherita**, just beyond the southern city walls.

CALENDAR OF EVENTS

Last weekend of January. **Arte Fiera** Dedicated to contemporary art, with exhibitions and events throughout the city.

February **Children's Carnival**. Floats and parades in the city centre

Early April **Children's Book Fair**, at Bolognafiere. The most important of its kind in the world.

Live Arts Week. Late April. Festival of Contemporary performing arts.

Madonna di San Luca Ascension Day. Heartfelt festival in honour of the icon of the Virgin in San Luca, with a procession through the city.

Future Film Festival Early May. International festival of cinema, animation and new technologies.

Diverdeinverde 3 days, late May. Private gardens in Bologna and surrounding hills open to the public.

Bè Bolognaestate June-September. Summer programme of music, art and theatre throughout the city.

Il Cinema Ritrovato Late June/early July. Celebration of film classics with screenings in various cinemas and on Piazza Maggiore.

Danzaurbana September. Contemporary dance festival.

Bologna, La Strada del Jazz Mid-September. Jazz concerts and events in the Quadrilatero.

Festa di San Petronio 4 October. Feast of the patron saint with concerts and other events taking place from 1st–4th October.

Bologna Jazz Festival October–November. Almost a month of concerts with well-known Italian and international jazz artists.

Gender Bender Late October/early November. International interdisciplinary festival dedicated to gender identity and sexual orientation.

Trekking Urbano Bologna Last weekend October. Guided tours to discover Bologna and surroundings.

Cioccoshow November. Five-day event dedicated to top-quality chocolate, with tastings, stalls, cooking lessons, etc.

Motor Show December. Showcasing cars and motorbikes manufactured in the region and elsewhere.

New Year's Eve 31 December. DJ music, street food and the burning of an effigy ('Vecchione') herald the New Year.

EATING OUT

It is not for nothing that the city is known as 'Bologna la Grassa' ('the fat one'). The city has 41 products protected by the European DOP (Designazione d'Origine Protetta) – more than any other city in Italy – an abundance of excellent restaurants, a tradition of long and leisurely meals and a spiralling number of cooking schools where visitors can learn the secrets of the local cuisine. It is generally regarded as the culinary capital of Italy. *Tortellini* remains the city's signature pasta dish, confirmed by an annual international cookery contest to determine the finest creations.

The regional cuisine is robust yet refined. Unless you fall for a tourist trap, it is a challenge to eat badly in Bologna and

PARMA – HAVEN OF GASTRONOMY

Crudo di Parma (Parma Ham and locally simply known as *prosciutto crudo*) and Parmigiano, the hard sharp-flavoured cheese, are intricately linked because the whey – the waste product from Parmigiano-Reggiano production – forms part of the quality fodder of the special pigs that produce Parma ham. True Parma ham is branded with the five-pointed crown of the medieval dukes of Parma and is produced in the Langhirino hills south of Parma. Here the raw hind thighs are hung in drying sheds for up to 10 months. The air that blows through the sheds is said to impart a sweet flavour to the meat – unlike cheap, mass-produced *prosciutto crudo* which is injected with brine and artificially dried to speed up the curing process. Try it as a starter, sliced into wafer-thin slivers for eating with bread, melon or figs. End your meal perhaps with slivers of superior Parmigiano-Reggiano, the king of Parmesans, which is especially delicious with apples, pears or a good red wine. To meet the master cheese-makers and taste their products visit www.parmigiano-reggiano.it.

Emilia-Romagna in general. The quality of ingredients is superb and local people are so demanding that mediocrity is punished. In the wealthy agricultural region of Emilia-Romagna each town produces its own pasta dishes and signature foods. Modena jealously guards the secrets of its world-renowned artisanal vinegar, Parma has patented Parmesan cheese and Italy's favourite ham (*prosciutto*

Tagliatelle alla bolognese

crudo di Parma) and the Ferrara area can only mean *cappellacci di zucca*, pumpkin-stuffed pasta, or *salama da sugo*, pig's liver and tongue stuffed into a pig's bladder and cured in wine.

The region is a trailblazer in creating food and wine routes (*Strade dei Vini e Sapori*). While these trails are often more of a promotional tool than a genuine excuse to tickle your taste buds, the routes are a convenient way to track down the top local producers of anything from asparagus and slippery eels to Parma ham and Parmesan cheese.

WHERE TO EAT

With gastronomic treats on offer in the Mercato di Mezzo, the ancient heart of the city, it is tempting to have snacks on the run. Here one of the many delis will make you up a *padina* or *crescentina* (flat focaccia-like bread) with a generous filling of finely sliced *prosciutto di Parma*, *mortadella* or *squacquerone* (fresh tangy cream cheese). Or you can choose from the enticing array of canapés and tapas-style food, including

Café life on Via Caprarie

fish, in the covered Mercato di Mezzo, which can either be taken away or consumed at casual communal tables.

Main meals are served in a **ristorante**, **trattoria** or **osteria** but the difference between the three is negligible these days. An **osteria**, traditionally a tavern or inn serving wine and pasta, can nowadays range from traditional to trendy (eg Modena's Osteria Francescana ranks among the world's top 5 restaurants). A **pizzeria** often extends to pasta and meat dishes but usually serves proper pizza bubbling hot from a wood-fired brick oven. The Italians prefer to eat pizza in the evening, and to accompany it with beer rather than wine. An **enoteca** or wine bar boasts a serious selection of fine wines, many available by the glass, and often served with a platter of cheese or charcuterie. Many inns or bars also serve food, especially pasta, and often have late-opening hours.

As in the rest of Italy, restaurants offer four courses: *antipasti* (hors d'oeuvres), the *primo* (first course, typically pasta in Emilia-Romagna but also risotto or soup), the *secondo* (main course of fish or meat) and the *dolce* (dessert), followed perhaps by cheese, coffee and a *digestivo*. Not that you would be expected, these days, to wade through every course.

ANTIPASTI

The most characteristic antipasto is a platter of assorted *salumi* –cured pork products such as wafer-thin slices of *prosciutto crudo di Parma* (Parma ham), *mortadella*, *salami*, *coppa di testa* (brawn), *cíccioli* (pork from Parma) and, if you're lucky, *culatello di Zibello*, one of the most prized and expensive of Italy's *salumi*, produced around Zibello, south of Parma. *Salumi* might be accompanied by a slice of crumbly Parmigiano-Reggiano cheese. Vegetable antipasti are likely to feature *peperoni* (peppers), *zucchini* (courgettes), *melanzane* (aubergine or eggplant) and *carciofi* (artichokes).

PRIMO

Tortellini, delicate parcels of pasta filled with pork, ham, *mortadella* and Parmesan cheese, is a tasty Bolognese speciality served typically *in brodo* (fragrant chicken broth) or simply with butter and Parmesan. Ideally the pasta will be handmade

FAR FROM BALONEY

If you think of Mortadella as the pre-packaged, pre-sliced and over-processed cold cut (American 'bologna sausage' or 'baloney') from your local supermarket, think again. Eating Mortadella di Bologna in its birthplace is a completely different experience. The pork is carefully selected according to strict regulation imposed by its PGI (Protected Geographical Indication), then finely ground and flavoured with small white flecks of high quality pork fat (from the neck of the pig), peppercorns and (sometimes) pistachios. It is then heat-cured for a few hours or several days according to the size. Sausages are typically between 5.5kg and 6.5kg (12 and 14 lbs) though in 1989 one was made that was over 5,75m (19ft) long, and 1,300kg (2,864 lbs) in weight. A good Mortadella should be sliced as thinly as possible and eaten with fresh, crusty bread along with a glass of light fruity red wine; alternatively you can have it as an appetiser in small diced cubes, as a creamy mousse with antipasti or as a stuffing for Bologna's famous *tortellini.* So popular is the pink sausage that there now a food festival in Bologna entirely devoted to it: the MortadellaBò in mid-October.

Tagliatelle tresses

Tagliatelle's origins go back to the 1487 wedding feast of Lucrezia Borgia and the Duke of Ferrara. The chef chosen to produce the lavish banquet included a new type of pasta, shaped in long golden strips, to reflect the blond tresses of the bride.

– you get 20 to 30 percent less filling if it's made with a machine. Other typical dishes are *tortellini* with ricotta and spinach and *tagliatelle* usually served with the true Bolognese sauce – and a far cry from what you get with 'spag bol'. *Ragù* is also used in the ubiquitous *lasagne*, another authentic dish of Bologna. Look out too for regional pastas such as *passatelli*, *cappelletti* ('little hats') or the bigger version: *cappellacci,* filled with pumpkin and Parmesan, and *anolini* ('rings') stuffed with beef, parmesan and breadcrumbs, and served in chicken broth.

SECONDI

Pork is the king of meats, served in variety of ways. Most menus will feature *cotellata alla bolognese*, a thin slice of pork (or veal cutlet) fried in breadcrumbs then baked with Parma ham and Parmesan cheese. *Bollito misto* (mixed boiled meats) is a stew of meats such as flank of beef, veal or ox tongue and Italian sausages, slowly simmered with celery, carrots and herbs and served with different sauces. *Fritto misto alla bolognese* is a mixed fry, varying from place to place but typically including potato croquettes, mozzarella, lamb, brains, zucchini, artichoke wedges, cauliflower florets and aubergine, all dipped in batter and deep fried. Some restaurants offer fresh fish but meat dominates the main courses. One of the best and most affordable places for fish and seafood is Banco 32 in the Mercato delle Erbe, next to the fishmonger. The seating is basic but the fish is brilliantly fresh, and there's a buzzy atmosphere.

DOLCI

Desserts range from a fruit salad or *gelato* to a choice of elaborate home-made desserts and cakes. Traditional desserts are *zuppa inglese* (the trifle-like 'English soup'), *tiramisu*, the alcoholic chocolate and coffee gateau from the Veneto, and *torta di riso,* a cake of rice, sugar, almonds and milk. Don't be surprised if you are offered gelato with a drizzle of balsamic vinegar. This should be the very superior Aceto Balsamico Tradizionale di Modena. It tastes much sweeter than ordinary Balsamic vinegar and can also be used in salads, drizzled over fresh berries or sometimes with honey over Parmigiano-Reggiano cheese. Aceto Balsamico in its pricey artisanal version bears no resemblance to the industrial liquid often found in supermarkets.

Local Mortadella for sale

GELATI

Greedy Bologna naturally excels at ice cream. As an alternative to a restaurant dessert you could do as many Bolognesi do and buy an ice cream from one of the superb *gelaterie*. The Bolognesi invariably disagree on which is best but firm favourites are **Sorbetteria Castiglione**, Via Castiglione 44 d/e, **Gelateria Ugo**, Via San Felice 24, **Gelatauro**, Via San Vitale 98 and **Cremeria Funivia** in Piazza Cavour.

Spag Bol?

It may seem surprising but one dish you won't find in Bologna is spaghetti bolognese. The *ragù alla bolognese*, which in its home town is a rich chunky blend of minced pork and beef, veg, wine, whole milk and tomato, is used to dress *tagliatelle*, never spaghetti.

WINES

The well-deserved reputation for good living in Emilia-Romagna is based more on food than wine. Huge amounts are produced but the quantity outweighs the quality. Nevertheless the wines have improved dramatically over the last two or three decades. Gone are the days of cheap, sweet, sparkling Lambrusco – at least in Italy. There are now some decent quality DOC dry (or off-dry), frothy Lambruscos with a pleasant acidity which goes well with the rich regional food. The Romagna side of the region, stretching east from Bologna to the coast, produces Sangiovese reds and the rather ordinary Trebbiano whites. Sangiovese varies enormously, from thin and tart to smooth dry, ruby red and full of flavour – but like Lambrusco it has seen a dramatic improvement. The best, such as Romagna DOC, completes with Italy's finest Sangiovese – and Sangiovese is Italy's most widely planted vine variety. Pignoletto, from the hills around Bologna and served throughout the city, is a delicate affordable white which goes well with antipasti and seafood. The sparkling form is a very popular *aperitivo*.

Restaurants invariably offer wines from other regions, such as Barolo from Piedmont or Brunello from Tuscany, while gourmet restaurants will also list a smaller selection of international wines. House wine, *vino della casa*, is normally acceptable and always reasonably priced. In cheaper places it's served in litre or half-litre carafes or jugs.

TO HELP YOU ORDER

A table for one/two/three **Un tavolo per una persona/ per due/per tre**

I would like... **Vorrei...**

The bill, please. **Il conto, per favore**

Do you have a set menu? **Avete un menù a prezzo fisso?**

I'd like a/an/some... **Vorrei...**

beer **una birra**	pepper **del pepe**
bread **del pane**	potatoes **delle patate**
butter **del burro**	salad **un'insalata**
coffee **un caffè**	salt **del sale**
fish **del pesce**	soup **una minestra**
fruit **della frutta**	sugar **dello zucchero**
ice cream **un gelato**	tea **un tè**
meat **della carne**	water **dell'acqua**
milk **del latte**	wine **del vino**

MENU READER

aglio garlic	**mela** apple
agnello lamb	**melanzane** aubergine
albicocche apricots	**merluzzo** cod
arancia orange	**ostriche** oysters
bistecca beefsteak	**pesca** peach
calamari squid	**pollo** chicken
carciofi artichokes	**pomodori** tomatoes
crostacei shellfish	**prosciutto** ham
fegato liver	**rognoni** kidneys
fiche figs	**tonno** tuna
formaggio cheese	**uovo** egg
frutti di mare seafood	**uva** grapes
funghi mushrooms	**verdure** vegetables
maiale pork	**vitello** veal
manzo beef	**vongole** clams

PLACES TO EAT

The price bands are based on a two-course meal including a glass of wine, service and cover charge.

€€€ = over €40 **€€** = €30–40 **€** = under €30

PIAZZA MAGGIORE AND AROUND

Ca' Pelletti € *Via Altabella 15 c/d; tel: 051-266 629; www.capelletti locandaitalia.it; daily 8am–10pm, Fri and Sat until 11pm.* A busy little *locanda*, catering for all tastes all day: lavish breakfasts (served until noon), lovely cakes, local pasta dishes (including vegetarian), *prosciutto*, salads and sweet and savoury *piadine* (sandwiches). Takeaway also available. Informal setting and welcoming atmosphere.

Da Gianni €€ *Via Clavature 18; tel: 051-229 43; www.trattoria-gianni. it; closed all day Mon and Sun pm and August.* Tucked down an alley in the 'foodie' quarter near San Petronio, this is one of Bologna's best trattorias, popular with locals. Menus are in Italian only but staff will help you choose from the Bolognese dishes. Try the melt-in-the-mouth *tortellini in brodo*, the *tagliatelle* or *gnocchi* with *ragù Bolognese* and the *bollito misto* (boiled meats – better than it sounds).

Eataly €–€€€ *Via degli Orefici 19; tel: 051-095 2820; www.eataly.it; Mon–Sat 8am–11.30pm, Sun 10am–11.30pm.* Part of the successful Eataly emporium, this is set inside a large bookshop with a variety of eating and drinking places on different floors. Excellent quality and choice and a popular spot for cocktails.

Enoteca Storica Faccioli €–€€ *Via Altabella 15b; tel: 051-349 300 2939; www.enotecastoricafaccioli.it; Mon–Wed 5pm–9.30pm, Thu–Fri noon–9.30pm, Sat 11am–10pm.* An historic, up-market wine bar with food, this place puts wine on a pedestal while serving unpretentious, genuine food, from cold cuts and cheeses to *crostini*, *lasagne* and *tortellini*.

Pane e Vino San Daniele € *Via Altabella 3a; tel: 051-296 0540; www. panevinospa.it; open daily noon–4pm and 6.30pm–12.30am.* This rustic, friendly place, part of an attractive Italian chain, is a central spot near the Cathedral for a light lunch of cold cuts, cheeses, pasta or a late-night revival over beer. Good value.

Pappagallo €€€ *Piazza della Mercanzia 3c; tel: 051-232 807;* www.alpappagallo.it; *closed Sun.* The Parrot (Pappagallo) is a charming old-world institution with fine dining, formal service and autographed photos of the many celebrities who have dined here (Sophia Loren, Gina Lollobrigida, Alfred Hitchcock, Frank Sinatra, Sharon Stone – just to name a few). The menu sticks strictly to Bolognese cuisine. If you haven't tasted the local *tortellini in brodo*, make this the place to try it. Reservations recommended.

Rodrigo €€€ *Via della Zecca 2/h; tel: 051-235 536;* www.ristoranterodrigobologna.it**;** *closed Sun.* In a palazzo formerly occupied by the National Mint, this is a long-established restaurant known for home-made pasta, fresh fish and variety of *funghi* in season (*porcini, chiodini, finferli* and more). Excellent choice of wines.

Trattoria Battibecco €€€ *Via Battibecco 4; tel: 051-223 298;* www.battibecco.com; *closed Sat lunch and Sun.* Splash out on creative dishes such as pumpkin and ginger risotto with marinated duck breast or lamb in pistachio crust with caramelised yellow onion; there are also Bolognese specialities, a good choice of fish and an excellent wine list. Tucked in an alley, close to Piazza Maggiore, it has a smart, stylish interior and professional staff. Popular with locals, reservations recommended.

EAST OF PIAZZA MAGGIORE

Clorofilla € *Strada Maggiore 64c; tel: 051-235 343;* www.ristorantenaturaleclorofilla.it; *closed Sun.* Bucking the Bolognese trend, the motto here is 'Eat your way to good health' and the dishes in this simple, wood-panelled restaurant are the perfect antidote to the rich and calorific local cuisine. Expect seitan steaks, couscous, tofu, vegetable drinks, vegan dishes and diverse salads.

Grassilli €€€ *Via dal Luzzo 3; tel: 051-222 961;* www.ristorantegrassilli.weebly.com; *closed all day Wed and Sun pm.* Close to the Two Towers this is an elegant and upmarket restaurant with the feel of an exclusive club. It was founded in 1944 and the many black and white photos (Luciano Pavarotti and Placido Domingo among them) recall the times when it was a popular haunt of opera singers. The cuisine is primarily Bolognese, but with a few French touches. Limited seating, booking recommended.

Scaccomatto €€€ *Via Broccaindosso 63; tel: 051-263 404; www. ristorantescaccomatto.com; closed Mon lunch.* If heavy Bolognese cuisine is taking its toll try Mario Ferrara's lighter dishes from southern Italy. Hailing from Basilicata, he has brought to the heart of Bologna an almost unheard of cuisine. His artfully-presented and often innovative dishes have proved very popular. Expect five- and six-course fish, meat or vegetable tasting menus.

UNIVERSITY QUARTER

Cantina Bentivoglio € *Via Mascarella 4b; tel: 051-265 416; www. cantinabentivoglio.it; daily 8pm-2am, closed Sun in summer and all of August.* Set in the lively university quarter this trusty tavern occupies the wine cellar of the noble Palazzo Bentivoglio. For over 50 years locals of all ages have been coming to soak up the live jazz, sound Bolognese food and informal atmosphere.

Trattoria/Pizzeria delle Belle Arti € *Via delle Belle Arti 14; tel: 051-225 581; www.belleartitrattoriapizzeria.com; open daily for lunch and dinner.* A family-run rustic trattoria serving local dishes as well as fish and paella, Calabrian cuisine and good pizzas from the wood-fired oven. Al fresco meals on the veranda in summer.

NORTH AND WEST OF PIAZZA MAGGIORE

Al Cambio €€-€€€ *Via Stalingrado 150; tel: 051-328 118; www. ristorantealcambio.it; closed Sun.* Set outside the city walls, close to the Fiera district, this gastronomic temple serves Bolognese favourites with a creative twist. Choose from either *the à la carte* or one of the tasting menus (€35 and €45 including wine, cover charge and coffee). It is popular with local gourmets and foodie tourists in the know. Smart setting, professional service.

Altro? € *Mercato delle Erbe, Via Ugo Bassi 23–25, tel: 351-014 4191; www.altrobologna.com, Mon–Fri 8am–11.30pm, Sat 8am–1am.* Within the revamped Mercato delle Erbe this is a new concept of a dozen or so outlets offering an array of high-quality simple food, sourced from the market: delicious pizza, veggie snacks, fish dishes, soups and salads. There is waiter service for lunch and dinner when there is more substantial fare on offer, otherwise it's self-service. At night it transforms to a cool spot for *aperitivos*.

Caminetto d'Oro €€ *Via de'Falegnami 4; tel: 051-263 494; www. caminettodoro.it; closed Sun.* This long-established family-run restaurant rustles up fine steaks and delicious desserts. Ingredients come fresh from the market and the bread and pasta is made in-house. There's also a well-stocked wine cellar. Very popular, especially in the evenings, so be sure to reserve a table.

Dal Biassanot €–€€ *Via Piella 16/a; tel: 051-230 644; www.dal biassanot.it; closed Sun and lunch on Mon.* Next door to the 'secret window' overlooking a canal, this is a warm, welcoming and very popular trattoria with top-notch local cuisine. Watch the *sfolgina* (pasta lady) rolling and cutting the pasta into perfect little shapes, then tuck into mouthwatering *tortellini rosa con pinoli e prosciutto* (pink tortelloni with pine nuts and Parma ham) or *tortelloni di ricotta burro e salvia* (with butter and sage), followed perhaps by roast rabbit or wild boar. If any space left, indulge in the chocolate cake with mascarpone cream.

Da Pietro €–€€ *Via de'Falegnami 18; tel: 051-648 6240; www.trattoria dapietro.it; closed Sun.* This welcoming, award-winning, family-run trattoria serves Bolognese, Emilian and Umbrian dishes from home-made pasta to grills, with truffles and mushrooms when the season permits. Summer terrace.

Del Rosso € *Via Augusto Righi 30; tel: 051-236 730; www.trattoriadel rosso.com; open daily lunch and dinner.* located between Via dell' Indipendenza and the university quarter, this is a cheap and unpretentious trattoria serving authentic Bolognese fare. Try the *crescentine* (savoury fried bread) with Parma ham, *mortadella* or *squacquerone* (fresh and tangy cream cheese) and wash it down with *vino sfuso* (wine on tap).

Ex Forno €–€€ *MAMbo, Via Don Minzoni 14/e; tel: 051-649 3896; www. exforno.com, Tue–Fri 7am–2am, Sat–Sun 10am–2am.* Come to see the art crowd in the modern MAMbo museum (see page 64). Decor combines vintage with the chic and contemporary. Daily specials, sumptuous salads, raw meats and fish are served at lunchtime, but it's particularly popular for the cocktails and the excellent *aperitivo* buffet (from 7pm) with the likes of *crescente* (focaccia-style bread), couscous and tempura vegetables. Sundays are popular for brunch.

Franco Rossi €€€ *Via Goito 3; tel: 051-238 818; www.ristorante francorossi.it; closed Sun.* Set just off busy Via dell'Indipendenza, this elegant and intimate spot serves classic Bolognese and Emilian cuisine with a lighter and creative touch. Choice of meat or fish menus, and a fine wine list.

Le Stanze €–€€ *Via Borgo San Pietro 1; tel: 051-228 767; www.le stanzecafe.com; daily 6pm–2am.* A bizarre but fashionable bar-restaurant set in a deconsecrated chapel in the Bentivoglio palace. The food is fine but cannot compete with the frescoes.

Serghei €€ *Via Piella 12; tel: 051-233 533; closed Sat and Sun.* Set in the city's secretive 'canal street', this homely Bolognese trattoria is strong on pasta dishes, especially *tortellini* and *tortelloni in brodo.* Popular too for cocktails.

Trattoria Da Me €–€€ *Via San Felice 50/A; tel: 051-555 486; http:// trattoriadame.com; closed Mon and Sun dinner.* Previously Da Danio, this historic and homely trattoria was reopened in 2016 by Elisa, granddaughter of the celebrated original owner Danio. Like her grandfather she produces authentic home-made Bolognese cuisine such as *tagliatelle al ragù, tortellini in brodo* and *cotoletta alla Bolognese* at affordable prices. Expect a warm welcome and a charming vintage setting.

Twinside €–€€ *Via de' Falegnami 6; tel: 051-991 1797; Mon–Sat 12.30pm–midnight.* Run by the owners of the neighbouring Caminetto d'Oro, this bistro, with an attractive modern interior, has tasty light modern Italian dishes along with Bolognese favourites. Beef tartare is a speciality, bread, pastry and ice-cream are all homemade. Excellent range of Italian wines by the glass.

SOUTH OF THE CENTRE

Biagi € *Via Saragozza 65; tel: 051-407 0049;* www.ristorantebiagi.it; *open evenings only, closed Tues.* This family-run restaurant, now in the third generation, has been welcoming clients since 1937. Come for authentic home-made Bolognese cuisine: *mortadella* mousse, *tortellini in brodo* or *tagliatelle al ragù,* followed perhaps by the *cotellata alla bolognese,* washed down with Sangiovese wine.

Drogheria della Rosa €€ *Via Cartoleria 10; tel: 051-222 529;* www.drogheriadellarosa.it; *open daily lunch and dinner.* One of Bologna's best-known trattorias, occupying an old pharmacy, still with its apothecary jars. The menu is short, the food simple but perfect. Pastas will include classic *tagliatelle* with *ragù* (meat sauce) and perhaps *tortelli* filled with *stracchino* and *squacquerone* cheeses with seasoned vegetables. Follow on with fillet steak in a dark sauce of aged balsamic vinegar from Modena.

Osteria de' Poeti €€ *Via de' Poeti 1b; tel: 051-236 166;* www.osteriadepoeti.com; *closed Sun and Mon.* This historic cellar-restaurant could be mistaken for a tourist trap but is equally popular with locals, enticed by the live music, the hearty regional cuisine and vast choice of wines. (Opt for the 'quiet room' if the music doesn't appeal). In the early 19th century the osteria was a haunt of poets and artists.

FERRARA

La Provvidenza €€ *Corso Ercole I d'Este 9;, tel: 0532-205 187;* www.ristorantelaprovvidenza.com; *closed Mon and dinner on Sun.* This leading restaurant has a gentrified rustic interior and offers a range of Ferrara specialities, from *pasticcio ferrarese* (pasta with a mushroom and meat sauce) to *fritto misto di carne* (mixed grill).

La Romantica €€ *Via Ripagrande 36; tel: 0532-765 957;* www.trattorialaromantica.com; *lunch and dinner daily.* A suitably romantic inn, set in the former stables of a 17th-century palace. Regional pasta dishes include *cappellacci di zucca,* with pumpkin, walnuts and sage; and *garganelli* with asparagus and mushrooms. Leave room for bangers-and-mash, Ferrara-style.

MODENA

Hosteria Giusti €€–€€€ *Via Farini 75; tel: 059-222 533;* www.hosteria
giusti.it; *Tue-Sat lunch only.* This little gem at the rear of a famous deli
favours meat, from roast suckling pig to cold cuts and fried *cotechino
di Modena* (pork sausage) with *zabaglione* sauce. Delicious home-
made pastas and desserts. Rustic but elegant, and very welcoming.

Osteria Francescana €€€ *Via Stella 2; tel: 059-223 912;* www.osteria
francescana.it; *Tue-Sat lunch and dinner.* The brainchild of master
chef Massimo Bottura, this osteria has three Michelin stars and
in 2015 was voted number two in The World's Best Restaurants.
Expect experimental, deconstructed versions of Italian classics.
Book a long time in advance and be prepared for a very hefty bill.

PARMA

La Greppia €€–€€€ *Strada Garibaldi 39a; tel: 0521-233 868;* www.
lagreppiaparma.com; *lunch and dinner daily.* THere you'll find the
very best of Parma-style cuisine, from *tortelli di erbette*, vegeta-
ble-stuffed pasta, to *culatello di Zibello*, the prized cured meat.

Trattoria del Tribunale €–€€ *Vicolo Politi 5; tel: 0521-285 527;* www.
trattoriadeltribunale.it; *lunch and dinner daily.* A welcoming and central but hard-to-find inn that serves *tortellini* stuffed with pumpkin
and herbs, or ricotta and spinach, naturally coated in Parmesan.

RAVENNA

Ca'De Ven € *Via Corrado Ricci 24; tel: 0544-30163;* www.cadeven.it;
Tue-Sun lunch and dinner. This 'house of wine', with long communal tables, serves regional wines with rustic fare based on *piadine*
(flat bread), cold cuts, cheese and, for dessert, caramelised figs.

La Gardela €–€€ *Via Ponte Marino 3; tel: 0544-217 147;* www.
ristorantelagardela.com; *Fri-Wed lunch and dinner.* This friendly inn
specialises in meat and fish grills as well as vegetable pasta dishes,
including mushrooms and truffles in season. Summer terrace.

A-Z TRAVEL TIPS

A Summary of Practical Information

A Accommodation . . . 116
   Airport 117
B Bicycle Hire 118
   Budgeting for
      your Trip 118
C Camping 119
   Car Hire 119
   Climate 120
   Clothing 120
   Crime 120
D Driving 121
E Electricity 122
   Embassies and
      Consulates 122
   Emergencies 123
G Gay and Lesbian
      Travellers 123
   Getting to Bologna . 123
   Guides and Tours . . 124
H Health and
      Medical Care 124

M Maps 125
   Media 126
   Money Matters 126
O Opening Times 127
P Police 127
   Post Offices 128
   Public Holidays 128
T Telephones 129
   Time Zones 129
   Tipping 129
   Toilets 130
   Tourist
      Information 130
   Transport 131
   Travellers with
      Disabilities 133
V Visas and Entry
      Requirements . . . 134
W Websites and
      Internet Access . . 134
Y Youth Hostels 135

A

ACCOMMODATION

Bologna has seen an increasing number of hotels and B&Bs in recent years, particularly those catering for tourists. However during the major trade fairs the accommodation is never sufficient and booking well in advance is crucial. Unless you are going specifically for a fair, these times are best avoided altogether, especially as hotel prices double or even treble. The main fairs are **Cosmoprof** (Cosmetics) in March, **Fiera del Libro per Ragazzi** (Children's Book Fair) in early April, **Cersaie** (ceramics) in late September and **Saie** (for the building industry) in mid-November. Finding a hotel room in the historic centre at other periods is generally not a problem. The quietest periods are the second week of January, February and mid-summer when it's very hot and many Bolognesi leave the city. Some restaurants may be closed for a couple of weeks or more in August.

Bologna has plenty of upmarket business hotels, many on the periphery of the city, but to have a true sense of the city stay in the historic centre even if it may mean paying more. Particularly appealing are the four 'Art hotels' (www.bolognaarthotels.it) that have cornered the market in seductive boutique hotels, all family-run, intimate, romantic hideaways. All occupy atmospheric palaces in the pedestrianised part of town and provide bikes for guests free of charge.

The centre has a good choice of B&B accommodation. Quality and price often compare favourably with 3-star hotels and any lack of amenities are more than compensated for by the personal welcome and the intimacy of the setting. B&Bs in the historic centre tend to be very small so early booking is essential. If you arrive on spec the Bologna Welcome tourist office (www.bologna welcome.com) will advise on available accommodation and will do the booking for you.

Prices vary depending on season and days of the week, as well as trade fairs. Substantial price reductions can be found in mid-winter, and also in July and August which are low season. Bear in mind however that locals tend to go away in August (though less so than previously) and quite a few restaurants are closed for a couple of weeks or more.

When making a reservation, a deposit of one night's stay, payable by credit card, is usually requested. Failure to inform the hotel in advance of cancellation will normally incur the loss of the deposit.

Beware of Bologna's tourist tax, introduced in 2012, which will add €1.50–5 per person per night to the cost of your room, depending on the rates. This has to be paid directly to your hotel at the end of your stay. Children under 14 are excluded from the tax.

I'd like a single/double room/twin beds **Vorrei una camera singola/matrimoniale/due letti singoli**
With bath/shower **con bagno/doccia**
What's the rate per night? **Quanto costa per notte?**

AIRPORT

Bologna's Guglielmo Marconi Airport (www.bologna-airport.it) is a mere 6km (4 miles) northwest of the city centre and has easy access. The Aerobus-BLQ shuttle service (http://aerobus.bo.it) provides a regular link with the city centre and Bologna Central Station. It runs daily from 5.30am to 12.15am, departs every 11 minutes, takes around 30 minutes and costs €6 for a single journey. Tickets can be bought at vending machines at the airport or railway station, at TPER ticket offices or online. For the city centre alight at Via dei Mille, the next and last stop is Bologna Central Station. Another shuttle service is Vivara Green (www.vivaraviaggi.it) that connects the airport to city hotels and needs to be pre-booked. Online bookings are accepted until noon of the day before the service (you fill in times of flights, name of hotel and pay in advance). For late reservations tel: (00 39) 051 760 622. The cost is €8 one way and the transfer time is around 30 minutes.

Taxis from the airport to the central station cost around €20–25 to the city centre, slightly more at night and on Sundays. The taxis at the airport have meters but it is always wise to check first on the approximate cost of your journey.

Taxis: Cotabo, tel: 051-372727; Radio Taxi, tel: 051-4590.

B

BICYCLE HIRE

In Bologna the uneven cobbled streets and ubiquitous pedestrian-only colonnades don't make for ideal cycling. Very few locals choose to cycle, even in the university quarter – a sharp contrast to Ferrara where cycling is a way of life. Bologna's historic centre is very compact and much of it pedestrianised, making it very easy to go by foot. But for those who prefer two wheels there is no shortage of bikes to hire. BIKEinBo (www.bikeinbo.it) charges €15 a day, €39 for three days (including helmet, locks, map and raincoat) and offers a free delivery and collection service. L'Altra Babele at Via Gandusio 10 (www.laltrababele.it), close to Bologna Central Station, charges €10 a day. A valid ID and deposit are required and there is no delivery service.

Prima Classe (tel: 051-855 2419) organises two-hour cycle tours in Bologna.

The tourist office has a leaflet of cycling trails around the city (or accessible at www.comune.bologna.it). A few hotels have free bikes for the use of guests.

BUDGETING FOR YOUR TRIP

Flights to Bologna with a low-cost carrier start at around €60 return from the UK in low season, but are more commonly

€120–250 return. Expect to pay €20 per person in a youth hostel, €120 upwards for a decent double room with bath or €100 in a simple hotel or B&B. Typically a three-course meal with wine costs from €30–40; a sandwich with a drink and coffee €8, coffee €1.50–€2.50; an *aperitivo* with nibbles or buffet included €10. Drinks at the bar are often cheaper than those served at a table. A metro or tram ticket is €1.30 if bought in advance, €1.50 if bought on the bus (exact cash required). Museum entrance charges range from €3–12. Entrance to state museums is free for EU citizens under 18 or over 65; and there is free for all entrance to state and some other museums on the first Sunday of the month. Look out for free concerts in churches, also free outdoor performances in summer.

C

CAMPING

The Campeggio Città di Bologna at the Centro Turistico Città (Via Romita 12/4a, tel: 051-325 016, www.hotelcamping.com) is close to the Fiera District but surrounded by greenery. A regular bus service links it to Bologna Central Train Station. Bungalows and mobile homes are available, as well as a restaurant, large swimming pool in summer (free of charge) and fitness centre (paying).

CAR HIRE

Most of Bologna's centre is closed to private traffic (see Driving) but you may want to hire a car to visit other cities of Emilia Romagna. The best rates are usually found online. The major rental companies have outlets at Bologna's G. Marconi airport. Hiring a small car costs €15–50 a day depending on the season. The cost includes third-party liability and taxes, but excludes insurance excess. Drivers must present their own national driving licence or one that is internationally recognised.

CLIMATE

Spring, early summer and early autumn are the best seasons to visit the city. The climate is hot and humid in summer, though the Apennine range can bring welcome breezes. Winters tend to be cold and wet, often with snow (particularly January and February). Lack of wind in winter also leads to fog and mist, often with high levels of air pollution. But there are also plenty of sunny days. A bonus of Bologna is the civilised system of porticoes allowing you to cross the city protected from rain and excessive heat.

	J	F	M	A	M	J	J	A	S	O	N	D
C°	6	9	13	18	21	25	27	27	24	19	13	8
F°	43	48	55	65	69	77	80	80	75	66	55	46

CLOTHING

Apart from the summer months, when all you need is light, cool clothes, bring plenty of layers, an umbrella and raincoat and in winter a warm coat or anorak. A pair of comfortable walking shoes is essential as you'll probably spend most of your time on foot. When visiting churches cover shoulders and don't wear skimpy attire.

CRIME

Take precautions against pickpockets. Leave important documents and valuables in the hotel safe, and keep a firm hold of handbags especially in crowded public areas and on public transport. For insurance purposes theft and loss must be reported immediately to the police.

I want to report a theft **Vorrei denunciare un furto.**
My wallet/passport/ticket has been stolen **Mi hanno rubato il portafoglio/il passaporto/il biglietto**

D

DRIVING

Bologna is at the crossroads of major motorways and can be reached directly from many major Italian cities. The A1 from Milan turns south at Bologna towards Florence, Rome and Naples; the A13 runs north to Ferrara and Padua; the A14 connects Bologna to Rimini and other coastal resorts on the Adriatic. Unless you are visiting sites outside Bologna a car is a positive drawback. The centre, which is a maze of one-way streets, is a mainly limited traffic zone (a 'ZTL') from 7am to 8pm daily, with access only for residents and authorised vehicles. In the so-called T area (via Ugo Bassi, Via Rizzoli and Via dell'Independenza) all traffic – even public transport and taxis – is forbidden at weekends, from 8am on Saturday to 10pm on Sunday. Entrance to the ZTL area is electrically monitored. Visitors staying in the city centre are allowed access but must provide their hotel or B&B with the car registration number in advance of arrival. Fines are imposed for those entering without a permit.

Driving assistance: Tel: 116

Parking. You can park in the blue lines, where price and times depend on the zones. Payment can be made with a smartphone or mobile. A list of car parks can be found on the www.bologna welcome.it website. If you are staying at a hotel or B&B in the centre you are allowed access but only by giving advance notice. Hotels in the city centre with parking facilities charge around €30 a night.

Rules of the road. Drive on the right, overtake on the left. Unless otherwise indicated, speed limits are 50kmh (30mph) in towns and built-up areas, 90kmh (55mph) on main roads and 130kmh (80mph) on motorways (*austostrade*). Headlights must be kept on during the day on motorways and state roads (*strade statali*). Seat belts are compulsory in the front and back, and children should be properly restrained. The use of hand-held mobile phones while driving is prohibited. The blood alcohol limit is 0.08 percent, and police occasionally make random breath tests.

Breakdown. In case of accident or breakdown call 113 (General Emergencies) or, for the Automobile club of Italy (ACI) 803 116 free from landline or mobile with Italian provider or 800 116 800 free from a mobile with a foreign provider. The ACI provides an efficient 24-hour service.

Where's the nearest car park? **Dov'è il parcheggio più vicino?**
Can I park here? **Posso parcheggiare qui?**
Fill it up please **Faccia il pieno per favore**
Unleaded/diesel **senza piombo/gasolio**
I've had a breakdown **Ho avuto un guasto**
There's been an accident **C'e stato un incidente**

E

ELECTRICITY
220V/50Hz AC is standard. Sockets take two-pin, round-pronged plugs. Visitors from the UK and the US will require an adaptor or transformer.

EMBASSIES AND CONSULATES
Australian Embassy, Via Antonio Bosio, 5, 00161 Rome, tel: 06-852 721, http://italy.embassy.gov.au

Canadian Embassy, Via Zara 30, 00198 Rome, tel: 06-854 441; www.canadainternational.gc.ca

Irish Embassy, Villa Spada, Via Giacomo Medici 1, 00153 Roma, tel: 06-585 2381; www.ambasciata-irlanda.it

Honorary consulate of South Africa, Via degli Agresti, 2, 40123 Bologna, tel: 051-272 600, www.sudafrica.it

Embassy of New Zealand, Via Clitunno, 44, 00198 Rome, tel: 06-853 7501, www.mfat/govt/nz

British Embassy, Via XX Settembre 80/a, 00187 Rome, tel: 06-4220 0001, www.gov.uk/government/world/organisations/british-embassy-rome

US Embassy, Via Vittorio Veneto 121, 00187 Rome, tel: 06-46741, http://rome.usembassy.gov

EMERGENCIES
Police 112, **Fire** 115, **Ambulance** 118, **General Emergency** 113

G

GAY AND LESBIAN TRAVELLERS
Bologna has a long tradition of openness towards diversity and minorities. Even in the 1970s, when very few Italian towns had openly gay-friendly bars or clubs, there were meeting places in the city for the LGBT community; and in 1995 Marcello Di Folco was elected Municipal Councillor of Bologna – the first transsexual in Europe to hold public office. The Igor Bookshop, Via S. Petronio Vecchio 3, is entirely devoted to LGBTQ culture.

The city is the seat of Arci Gay, Italy's biggest gay-rights organisation at Via Don Minzoni 18, tel: 051-0957 200. This is also home to the Cassero LGBT Centre, the provincial branch of Arci Gay and venue of Il Cassero, one of the city's most popular gay and lesbian clubs.

LGBT information, including services, associations and gay-friendly bars and clubs, can be found on the tourist information website (www.bolognawelcome.com).

GETTING TO BOLOGNA
Bologna is well connected to the major cities of Europe. From the

UK direct flights to Bologna are operated by British Airways (www. britishairways.com) who fly from London Heathrow, easyJet (www. easyjet.com) from London Gatwick and Ryanair (www.ryanair.com) from Stansted and Edinburgh. Flight costs vary according to the time of year and day of the week. An off-season return booked in advance with a low-cost carrier can be as little as €60 (hand-luggage only).

There are no direct flights from North America to the city but you can change at one of the European hubs (Rome, Milan, Paris, Frankfurt or Zurich).

GUIDES AND TOURS

Two-hour walking tours of the city depart daily from the Bologna Welcome tourist office in Piazza Maggiore. In Italian and English, the guided tours take in the Basilica of San Petronio, the ancient market area, the Two Towers and other cultural highlights of the historic centre. (€14 per person and free for children under 12).

Bologna Welcome offers a host of other guided tours, both within the city and in the province of Emilia-Romagna. Many of these are gastro-themed, eg the food stores of the medieval market, San-giovese wine tours, a visit to a Parmigiano Reggiano cheese factory, a truffle factory or a tour of Modena's prestigious balsamic vinegar production. Motor aficionados can test drive a Ferrari, visit the two Ferrari museums and see the Ducati and Lamborghini factory floors and historical collections.

Il Salotto di Penelope (www.ilsalottodipenelope.it) is one of the city's 25 cookery schools where you can learn the secrets of making Bolognese pastas and other Emilian specialities.

H

HEALTH AND MEDICAL CARE

All EU countries have reciprocal arrangements for reclaiming the costs of medical services. UK residents should obtain the EHIC (European Health Insurance Card), available from post offices or online at www.gov.uk/european-health-insurance-card. This does not cover emergency repatriation costs or additional expenses. To cover all eventualities a travel insurance policy is advisable, and for non-EU residents essential. For insurance claims keep all receipts for medical treatment and any medicines prescribed.

The water is safe to drink but most locals drink mineral water.

If you need a doctor (*medico*), ask at a pharmacy or your hotel. For serious cases or emergencies dial 118 for an ambulance or head for the *Pronto Soccorso* (Accident and Emergency) of the local hospital which will also deal with emergency dental treatment.

Pharmacies. A pharmacy is identified by a green cross. Locations of pharmacies which are open after-hours are posted on all pharmacy doors. An all-night service is available at the Farmacia Comunale at Piazza Maggiore 6 in the centre of the city.

I need a doctor/dentist **Ho bisogno di un medico/dentista**
Where is the nearest chemist? **Dov'è la farmacia più vicina?**

M

MAPS

The Bologna Welcome tourist office at the airport or in Piazza Maggiore supply a useful free and updated map of the city.

You are unlikely to need anything more detailed but if you require maps for other cities or areas of Emilia Romagna you can find them at La Feltrinelli international bookshop by the Due Torri (Via Zamboni, 7).

MEDIA

Most hotels in Bologna will provide satellite TV, broadcasting 24-hour English-speaking news channels. The Italian state TV network, RAI (Radiotelevisione Italiana) broadcasts three channels, RAI 1, 2 and 3, and a huge number of private channels pouring out soaps, films and quiz shows. The state-run radio stations (RAI 1, 2 and 3) mainly broadcast news, chat and music.

The most useful English-language magazine is *L'Ospite di Bologna* (A Guest of Bologna) with full listings and other practical information. It is published fortnightly in Italian and English and is available in upmarket hotels and (usually) the tourist office. Alternatively details of events are available on the Bologna Welcome website, www.bolognawelcome.com.

National dailies such as the *Corriere della Sera* and *La Repubblica* have Bologna sections, and *Il Resto del Carlino* (www.ilrestodel carlino.it) is almost entirely devoted to Bologna, including listings (in Italian). The main English and foreign newspapers are available on the day of publication from major newsstands.

MONEY MATTERS

Currency. In common with most other European countries, the official currency used in Italy is the euro (€), divided into 100 cents. Euro notes come in denominations of 500, 200, 100, 50, 20, 10 and 5; coins come in denominations of 2 and 1, then 50, 20, 10, 5, 2 and 1 cents.

Exchange facilities. Banks offer the best rates, followed by exchange offices (cambi) and hotels. Some exchange offices offer commission-free facilities, but check that the exchange rate is not exorbitant. They are usually open Mon–Sat 8.30am–7.30pm. Both the airport and railway station have exchange offices.

Credit cards and cash machines. The major international credit cards are accepted in the majority of hotels, restaurants and stores.

I want to change some pounds/dollars **Desidero cambiare delle sterline/dei dollari**
Can I pay with a credit card? **Posso pagare con la carta di credito?**

O

OPENING TIMES

Banks generally open Monday–Friday 8.30am–1.30pm and 2.30–4pm, but hours vary; some open continuously from 8am–4pm.

Museums and art galleries. Opening times vary but closing day is nearly always Monday. Some museums close over the lunch period or close early, eg at 2pm or 3pm. The tourist office on Piazza Maggiore has up-to-date lists of opening hours for museums, galleries and churches.

Churches usually close from noon to 3pm or later, though San Petronio is open all day.

Shops are open Monday to Saturday, and many are also open on Sundays. Opening hours are traditionally 9am–1pm and 3.30–7.30pm but many shops are now open all day. Some shops close for at least a part of August.

P

POLICE

The city police or *Polizia Urbana* regulate traffic and enforce laws while the *Carabinieri* are the armed military police who handle law and order. In an emergency the Carabinieri (Via dei Bersaglieri 3)

Where's the nearest police station? **Dov'è il posto di polizia più vicino?**

can be reached on 112 – or you can ring the general emergency number, 113. In the case of stolen goods, contact the Questura (police station) at Piazza Galileo, 2B, tel: 051-640 1577.

See also Emergencies.

POST OFFICES

The central post office, at Piazza Minghetti 4, is open Mon–Fri 8.20am–7.05pm, Sat 8.20am–12.35pm. Most other post offices open Mon–Fri 8.20am–1.35pm, Sat 8.20am–12.35pm. Stamps can be purchased at any post office but it is faster and easier to buy them from a *tabaccheria*.

Where's the nearest post office? **Dov'è il l'ufficio postale più vicino?**
I would like a stamp for this letter/postcard **Desidero un francobollo per questa lettera/cartolina**

PUBLIC HOLIDAYS

1 January *Capodanno* New Year's Day
6 January *Epifani (La Befana)* Epiphany
25 April *Festa della Liberazione* Liberation Day
1 May *Festa dei lavoratori* Labour Day
2 June *Festa della Repubblica* Republic Day
15 August *Ferragosto* Assumption
4 October *San Petronio*
1 November *Ognissanti* All Saints' Day
8 December *L'Immacolata Concezione* Immaculate Conception
25 December *Natale* Christmas Day
26 December *Santo Stefano* St Stephen's Day
Moveable dates:
Pasqua Easter
Lunedì di Pasqua Easter Monday

T

TELEPHONES

When phoning abroad, dial the international code, followed by the city or area code and then the number. Note that telephone numbers within Italy are usually 9 or 10 digits long but can be any amount of digits from 6–11. Numbers beginning with 800 are free. Italian area codes are incorporated into the numbers, so even if calling within Bologna you must include the code.

Some mobiles phones need to be activated with a roaming facility or be 'unblocked' for use abroad. Check with your mobile company before leaving home. If you are in Italy for some time it's worth purchasing an Italian SIM 'pay as you go' (*scheda pre-pagata*) available from any mobile shop in Italy. To do so you will need your passport or ID card.

TIME ZONES

Italy is one hour ahead of Greenwich Mean Time (GMT). From the last Sunday in March to the last Sunday in October, clocks are put forward by one hour. The chart below shows times across the globe when it is midday in Bologna.

New York	London	**Bologna**	Jo'burg	Sydney
6am	11am	**noon**	1pm	8pm

TIPPING

A 10 percent service charge is normally included in a the restaurant bill and a tip on top of this is not expected. Most restaurants still impose an outdated cover and bread charge (*pane e coperto*) of around €1.50–5. For quick service in bars leave a coin or two with your till receipt when ordering. Taxi drivers do not expect a tip but always appreciate a bit extra.

Thank you, this is for you **Grazie, questo è per lei**
Keep the change **Tenga il resto**

TOILETS

The train and bus stations have public toilets, so does the Biblioteca Salaborsa on Piazza di Nettuno right in the centre. Otherwise it is generally a case of using the facilities of a café or bar. To avoid embarrassment, remember that *Signori* is Men, *Signore* is Women.

Where are the toilets, please? **Dov'è sono i gabinetti, per favore?**

TOURIST INFORMATION

Italian Tourism authority offices abroad:
Australia: Level 2, 140 William Street, East Sydney NSW 2011, tel: 02-9357 2561, www.enit.it
Canada: 110 Yonge St #503, Toronto, ON M5C 1T4, Canada, tel: 416-925 4882, www.enit.it
UK: 1 Princes Street, London W1B 2AY, tel: 020-7408 1254, www.italiantouristboard.co.uk
US: **New York**: 686 Park Avenue, 3rd Floor, New York, NY 10065, tel: 212-245 5618
Chicago: 3800 Division Street, Stone Park, IL 60165, tel: 312-644 0996
Los Angeles: 10850 Wilshire Blvd, Suite 575, Los Angeles, CA 90024, tel: 310-820 1898.
The common website for US offices is www.italia.it
Bologna Tourist Offices
The main Bologna Welcome tourist office (tel: 051-350 853, open Mon–Sat 9am–7pm, Sun 10am–5pm) is in the heart of the city

under the portico of Palazzo Podestà in Piazza Maggiore. Services include hotel booking, restaurant reservation, bookings for guided tours or tickets for flights, trains, theatre, cultural and sporting events. Staff are efficient and helpful and can supply free maps and leaflets in English. There is a second Bologna Welcome Office in the Arrivals' Hall of Bologna's G. Marconi airport and a third operates in the Fiera trade centre during exhibitions. Bologna Welcome has an excellent, up-to-date website, www.bolognawelcome.com, which gives you everything you need to know for a stay in the city from descriptions of hotels, restaurants and museums to where to go for an *aperitivo* or how to use the buses. Use the search box to make the most of it. The Bologna Welcome Card, available at both Bologna Welcome offices, allows you free admission to many museums, discounts at restaurants and shops and a return BLQ airport shuttle bus ticket. It is good value at €20.

The Mibac Call centre (Ministry of cultural heritage and activities) is available in English, Spanish and Italian, free phone: 800 99 11 99.

TRANSPORT

The historic centre, where virtually all the attractions are located, is compact, flat and easily covered on foot. It is easy to find your way around with a free map from the tourist office, colonnades giving shelter from the elements and towers providing useful landmarks.

Bus. Bologna has a good public transport network run by TPER (www.tper.it) and covering the whole city and beyond. Routes and timetables are available on the TPER website. Tickets can be bought in advance from tobacconists, newsstands or from one of the five TPER information points in the city. A single ticket, which is valid for 75 minutes, costs €1.30 if bought in advance or €1.50 if bought on the bus (you need the exact change). Tickets bought before boarding must be validated as soon as you board the bus. A 24-hr ticket with unlimited bus travel costs €4, or a city pass for 10 journeys costs €12 and can be used by more than one person.

The coach station is located just 100m/yards from Bologna Central Train Station. Coach services connect Bologna with main Italian cities though trains tend get you there faster.

The City Red Bus (www.cityredbus.com) is an open-top bus operating daily, with an audioguide providing information en route in eight languages. 'Stop and Go' tickets are valid all day. The Bologna Welcome office in Piazza Maggiore sells tickets; alternatively you can buy them on board or at affiliated stores and hotels. The same company also runs the San Luca Express that connects the centre to the Basilica of San Luca, in season only.

Rail. Bologna central train station (Piazza Medaglie d'Oro 2, www.bolognacentrale.it) is a key hub in the Italian rail network with high-speed trains connecting the city to Florence (30 minutes), Milan (one hour), Venice (1.5 hours) and Rome (2.5 hours). Trains are also the most efficient means of transport to cities of Emilia Romagna: Modena, Ferrara, Parma, Rimini and Ravenna. Pick up a copy of *Un Ospite di Bologna* (Guest of Bologna) magazine (free from hotels) to check the train times to places close to Bologna. For complete online timetables and booking (in English or Italian) contact www.trenitalia.com.

The station is located about 20 minutes' walk from the historic centre on the northern edge of the city. There are two main train companies, Trenitalia and Italo, both offering trains out of Bologna Centrale. The ticket office is open 6am–9pm; alternatively you can purchase tickets online or at the self-service vending machines. Tickets must be validated at the yellow machines in the station. If you have a return ticket you must validate it twice (once going, once returning).

Taxis. Taxis cannot be hailed in the street. The main ranks are at

Bologna Central Station and Piazza Maggiore but there are others scattered through the city. Taxis have meters but it is always wise to agree an approximate cost with the driver before setting off. The fare will depend on the time of day, the day of the week and the number of pieces of luggage.

The following radio taxi companies offer a 24 hour service:

Cotabo: 051-372 727

Cat: 051-4590

Cosepuri Auto Blu: 051-519 090

When's the next bus/train to…? **Quando parte il prossimo autobus/treno per…?**
single (one-way) **andata**
return **andata e ritorno**
What's the fare to..? **Qual'è la tariffa per…?**

TRAVELLERS WITH DISABILITIES

Cobblestones and stairways within palazzi are disincentives for travellers with disabilities but there is now access in most public buildings and main museums. The Bologna Welcome website (www.bolognawelcome.com, under Tourist Guide/Practical Info section) has useful information for the disabled such as public and private transportation, free parking, accommodation, restaurants and useful links. The office also provides a handy map, *Bologna, A City for Everyone*, which marks routes for travellers with disabilities including written itineraries with full details of the easiest access, where to find lifts, etc. A special Radio-Taxi service (tel: 051-372 727) operates 24 hours for those in wheelchairs or those who need special assistance. Vehicles serving disabled persons can circulate in the ZTL (Restricted Traffic Zone) provided notice of the registration number can be given to the hotel or B&B in advance to pass on to the Municipality. In the case of access which is not previously communicated, details can be sent within 48 hours of entering the controlled area. Information in Italian only is available on the website of the Settore Mobilità, www.comunebologna.it/trasporti. Vehicles used for the disabled are not subject to parking fees.

Accessibol is an app to find accessible places in Bologna – with useful links. Alternatively contact Accessible Italy (www.accessible italy.com), a non-profit making organisation which helps foreign tourists with disabilities to plan their holidays in Italy.

V

VISAS AND ENTRY REQUIREMENTS

EU citizens need only a valid passport. Citizens of the US, Canada, Australia and New Zealand can stay for up to three months without a visa, and can extend their stay with a visa from the Italian embassy or consulate.

Residents of non-EU countries can claim a refund for part of VAT (IVA in Italy) on purchases of more than €155 at stores participating in the VAT-refund scheme. Reclaim the VAT at the airport.

W

WEBSITES AND INTERNET ACCESS

www.bolognawelcome.com – official city tourist website, packed with information.

www.bologna-airport.it – Bologna airport information.

www.trenitalia.com – train information.

www.tper.it – bus information.

www.emiliaromagnaturismo.it – official website for the whole region, in both Italian and English with useful links.

www.cittadarte.emilia-romagna.it – for all the region's art cities.

www.turismo.comune.parma.it – Parma tourist information.
www.ferrarainfo.com – Ferrara tourist information.
www.visitmodena.it – Modena tourist information.
www.turismo.ra.it – Ravenna tourist information.
www.visit-rimini.com – Rimini tourist information.

To find free WiFi hotspots (indoor and outdoor) go to the Iperbole Wireless Network website (www.comune.bologna.it/wireless). The map is constantly updated.

In the city centre the tourist office on Piazza Maggiore, the archaeological museum and the Biblioteca Salaborsa are all WiFi hotspots. The Salaborsa has free internet access for 30–60 minutes.

Hotels generally include WiFi in the room rates. An increasing number of cafés and restaurants provide WiFi, with purchase of food or a drink, especially in the university quarter.

Y

YOUTH HOSTELS

Contact your national youth hostel association before departure to obtain an international membership card. The best hostel is the **Ostello We_Bologna**, Via de' Carracci 69/14, hello@we-bologna.it or www.hostelworld.com, tel: 051-039 7900, a highly-rated design hostel 800m/yards northwest of the station. Rooms which accommodate two or four people all come with en suite bathroom and air conditioning. Communal areas include kitchen, breakfast and lounge, video room and outdoor area. 24-hour reception, free WiFi. Prices from €20 per person, breakfast €3.50 per day.

A cheaper alternative is the **Due Torri-San Sisto**, Via Viadagola, 5, tel: 051-501 810 (www.hihostels.com) but this is located 6km (4 miles) northeast of the city, a 30-minute bus ride from the centre. It is modern, functional and surrounded by greenery. Accommodation consists of singles, doubles and rooms for 3, 4 or 5.

RECOMMENDED HOTELS

Bologna has a wide range of accommodation from the large modern hotels on the periphery aimed at business travellers to the smaller hotels and B&Bs in the historic centre, which have far more appeal for tourists. Bologna is a city for all seasons but during the main trade fairs hotels can be booked up months in advance and prices double or often treble. Prices tend to fall in mid-summer and are generally at their cheapest in February, the quietest month. If you arrive without a reservation the Bologna Welcome tourist office (www.bologna welcome.com) in Piazza Maggiore offers a free hotel-booking service.

Hotels are officially categorised from one-to-five stars, or, at the very top end of the scale, five-star deluxe. The stars assigned denote facilities (which sometimes don't exist) and are no real indicator of charm or atmosphere. The most prestigious hotel is undeniably the five-star deluxe Grand Hotel Majestic. Some of the most appealing hotels, right in the centre and integrating seamlessly into the medieval context, are the Bologna Art Hotels, a chain of four: The Commercianti, Orologio, Novecento and Corona d'Oro (www.bolognarthotels.it). They also have a handful of centrally-located four- and five-star apartments available. B&Bs in Bologna are now plentiful but because of space restrictions in the city centre many of them only have one or two rooms.

Hotel rates usually include breakfast, though check first as a few hotels have started to charge it separately. Being Bologna, breakfast is usually a fairly substantial fare including a spread of fresh fruit, Parma ham, cheeses, yoghurts and freshly baked patisserie. If breakfast is not included in the room rate it is usually better value to pop out for a cappuccino and croissant in the local café.

As is the case in many of Italy's cities a tourist tax applies to any non-resident staying in a hotel or B&B. The tax was introduced in Bologna in 2012. Children under 14 are exempt. The rate is €1.50–5 per person per night depending on the room rate, for up to a maximum of five nights. For a couple staying in a 4-star hotel for three nights there would be an extra cost of around €15. The tax must be paid to the hotel before departure (it is never paid in advance either to the hotel or to a tour operator or hotel website).

As a basic guide the symbols below indicate rack rates per night for standard double room including VAT, service and breakfast, but excluding tourist tax.

€€€€	over 300 euros
€€€	200–300 euros
€€	120–200 euros
€	under 120 euros

PIAZZA MAGGIORE AND AROUND

Art Hotel Commercianti €€-€€€ *Via de'Pignattari 11; tel: 051-745 7511*; www.art-hotel-commercianti.it. Set in a side street beside San Petronio, this frescoed medieval palace is home to a stylish yet seductive hotel in the very heart of the city. Well-restored public rooms lead to romantic bedrooms under the eaves, many of which have views across the alley to the Gothic windows of San Petronio or over the rooftops. Best rooms are at the top. Excellent buffet breakfast and free bikes.

Art Hotel Corona d'Oro 1890 €€-€€€ *Via Guglielmo Oberdan 12; tel: 051-745 7611*; www.hco.it. On a cobbled, traffic-free street close to the famous two towers, this delightful, peaceful hotel is one of the most sought-after city-centre retreats. An atmospheric medieval palazzo, it is said to have housed Italy's first printing works, and has been offering accommodation and a warm welcome since it first opened in 1890. A Renaissance portico, 16th-century coffered ceilings and the former winter garden, transformed into an elegant entrance hall, all add to the charm.

Art Hotel Novecento €€-€€€ *Piazza Galileo 4/3; tel: 051-745 7338*; www.bolognarthotels.it. A chic and glamorous designer hotel in art nouveau style right in the centre of the city. Guest rooms, which include suites, overlook historic corners of the medieval centre.

Art Hotel Orologio €€-€€€ *Via IV Novembre 10; tel: 051-745 7411*; www.bolognarthotels.it. This small, family-run, three-star hotel is much in demand for its unbeatable location beside Piazza Maggiore and for its old-world charm. Some rooms have views of the medieval Due Torri and the heart of historic Bologna.

Ca' Fosca Due Torri €€ *Via Caprarie 7; tel: 051-261 221; mobile: (00 39) 335 314761; www.cafoscaduetorri.com.* Set in the shadow of the medieval Due Torri this is a gem of a B&B, boasting a gracious art nouveau inspired interior and views of city towers and domes. Patrizia is a font of city knowledge and an exceptionally welcoming, extrovert and helpful hostess. Amenities include a library, guest kitchen and a winter garden where breakfast is served. Studios also available.

Cappello Rosso €€€€ *Via de Fusari 9; tel: 051-261 891; www.alcappello rosso.it.* Luxury hotel in the centre, set in a former tavern that was renowned for its roast partridge. There are 33 rooms, each one different, but all contemporary, sleek and equipped with luxuries such as big-screen TVs and silk kimonos. Designer rooms include: the Silent Cage Room 4'33", dedicated to the American composer John Cage, the Shock in Pink room, which pays homage to Schiaparelli's surreal universe and Lettera 305, dedicated to the old Lettera 22 typewriter (with a gigantic keyboard on the ceiling).

Centrale € *Via della Zecca 2; tel: 051-006 3937; www.albergocentrale bologna.it.* One of Bologna's best two-star hotels: central, with clean and simple rooms in classic-style, excellent continental breakfast and staff who go out of their way to help. Rooms are on the third and fourth floor (with lift) of an 18th-century palazzo with fine views over the rooftops.

Delle Drapperie €–€€ *Via delle Drapperie 5; tel: 051-223 955; www. albergodrapperie.com.* Small and charming B&B in the heart of the bustling Mercato di Mezzo. Pretty rooms come in art nouveau style, all in different colours with lovely floral designs and antiques. Four junior suites overlook the rooftops.

Roma €€–€€€ *Via d'Azeglio 9; tel: 051-226 322; www.hotelroma. biz.* The location of the Roma is hard to beat: on a smart pedestrianised street, popular for shopping and *la passeggiata* (evening stroll) just a few steps away from the Piazza Maggiore. The hotel has a civilised atmosphere, traditional rooms and personal service. Emilian specialities are served in the C'era Una Volta restaurant.

Torre Prendiparte €€€€ *Piazzetta Prendiparte; tel: 051-589 023;* www.prendiparte.it. A unique opportunity to rent your own 60m (197ft)-high medieval 900-year-old tower with a panoramic terrace (12 floors to climb). This is a romantic retreat – accommodation is for one couple only. The living areas with bedroom, kitchen and sitting room, take up three floors. All requirements are catered for including a private chef for a candlelit dinner. Popular for special occasions or a romantic and exclusive B&B for two. This unique experience comes of course with a high price tag.

UNIVERSITY QUARTER

Casa Ilaria € *Largo Respighi 8; tel: 051-412 4760;* www.casailaria. com. Very handy for the Teatro Comunale (main venue for opera, concerts and ballet), this is a quiet and welcoming B&B with spacious rooms and garden views. Tiziana is a gracious host and very helpful with information on the city and advice on local restaurants. Continental breakfasts come with delicious home-made cake – or there are eggs and bacon on request. The hosts also hold cookery courses and organise gourmet tours.

NORTH AND WEST

4 Viale Masini €–€€ *Viale A. Masini 4/3; tel: 051-242 811;* www.4viale masini.com. Design hotel with well-conceived rooms, chic public places and a fresh, contemporary feel. It's certainly handy for the station but on a busy main road, 15–20 minutes' walk from Piazza Maggiore.

B&B Bologna nel Cuore €€ *Via Cesare Battisti 29; tel: 051-269 442;* www.bolognanelcuore.it. Expect a warm welcome and expert local knowledge from Maria Ketty, who has been running this B&B for 10 years. There are two attractively decorated and well-equipped double rooms and two apartments with cooking facilities.

Break 28 € *Via Marconi 28; tel: 333-331 3560;* www.break28.com. Apartment on the top floor of a tower block with a minimalist designer interior to match the Frank Lloyd Wright-inspired exterior. The location is central between the historic centre and the station, yet with views over the city hills towards San Luca. Friendly, helpful owners.

Cavour €–€€€ *Via Goito 4; tel: 051-228 111;* www.cavour-hotel.com. This friendly and professionally-run three-star has an excellent location in a side street just off Via dell'Independenza, with plenty of good places to eat nearby. The 38 rooms vary in size and style from standard and superior to the newly furbished deluxe rooms, available with jacuzzis.

Grand Hotel Majestic €€€€ *Via dell'Indipendenza 8; tel: 051-225 445;* www.grandhotelmajestic.hotelsbologna.it. In a former 18th-century seminary, the hotel lives up to its name and provides a rendezvous for the most affluent Bolognese, many of whom come to dine in its prestigious restaurant I Carracci. Many a Hollywood legend has stayed here. Public rooms retain their former splendour: frescoed walls, moulded ceiling and grand chandeliers. Guest rooms combine classical charm and contemporary luxury and palatial suites are furnished with antiques and marble bathrooms with jacuzzis.

Il Guercino € *Via Luigi Serra; tel: 051-369 893;* www.guercino.it. This is a discreet, classic hotel in a quiet (although unfashionable) area 5 minutes' walk from the station, 20 plus to the historic centre. Rooms are comfortable and good value, though some are on the small side. Friendly, helpful staff and good breakfasts.

I Portici €€€–€€€€ *Via dell'Indipendenza 69; tel: 051-42185;* www.iporticihotel.com. This restored art nouveau palazzo is a four-star deluxe hotel and member of SLH group, Small Luxury Hotels of the World. The chic minimalist interior was the work of leading Italian and international designers. Guest rooms have parquet floors, pastel shades and, in the case of the deluxe rooms, original art nouveau frescoes. Rooms look out on to the park or Via dell'Independenza, a main shopping street. The I Portici Restaurant is one of the best in the city.

Metropolitan €€ *Via dell'Orso 6; tel: 051-229 393*; www.hotel metropolitan.com. The location between the city centre and the station combined with a fresh, contemporary Far Eastern decor make the Metropolitan a popular choice both for business travellers and tourists. Book well in advance for the cool new apartments at the top.

Royal Carlton €€€–€€€€ *Via Montebello 8; tel: 051-249 361;* www. royalhotelcarltonbologna.com. This austere-looking tower near the station contains a grand hotel with helpful staff, large comfortable bedrooms and hotel parking. The professional ambience and convenient location five minutes' walk from the station and 10 from the historic centre make it a popular choice for executives and tourists alike. Inside the emphasis is on space, modern comforts and cool efficiency.

Touring €€ *Via De' Mattuiani 1; tel: 051-584 305;* www.hoteltouring.it. Friendly, family-run three-star hotel with a panoramic roof terrace looking onto the city and San Luca in the distance. Guest rooms vary from the older classic-style to the newly renovated contemporary rooms and spacious suites. In the summer months guests can enjoy the jacuzzi on the rooftop. Ten minutes' walk from Piazza Maggiore.

UNA Hotel €€ *Viale Pietramellara 41/43; tel: 051-60801;* www.una hotels.it. Right in front of the station this is a modern design hotel and part of the Italian UNA chain. Chic, clean lines set off colourful panels and minimalist furniture makes for pleasantly uncluttered rooms. Offers some good deals off season (but not during trade fairs).

SOUTH

Antica Casa Zucchini €€ *Via Santo Stefano 36; tel: 3479 110731;* www. anticacasazucchini.it. This charming B&B near the church of Santo Stefano occupies an historic house, parts of which date back to the mid-15th century. Features include a portico with Istrian stone capitals, grand 18th-century staircase and frescoed ceilings and antiques in the three bedrooms.

Il Convento dei Fiori di Seta €€ *Via Orfeo 34/4; tel: 051-272 039*; www.ilconventodeifioridiseta.com. Converted from a nunnery dating back to the 15th century, this little boutique hotel on the southern edge of the city has plenty of personality. Original features, such as vaulted rooms, frescoes and sacred altar sculptures have been retained but there's a nod to the modern era with chic contemporary lighting and seating, and mosaic tiled bathrooms. Four of the guest rooms have been fashioned out of the aisle and apse of the church, six are on the upper floor, individually designed in contemporary style.

Porta San Mamolo €€–€€€ *Vicolo Del Falcone 6/8; tel: 051-042 0456*; www.hotel-portasanmamolo.it. This welcoming and very accommodating B&B is near the Porta San Mamolo on the southern edge of the city, 10–15 minutes' walk from the centre, with the advantage of a pretty courtyard garden for breakfasts in summer. Rooms, in traditional style (either doubles, triples or suites), are a good size and some have their own terrace.

Porta Saragozza € *Viale Carlo Pepoli 26; tel: 051-644 7437*; www.portasaragozza.it. This charming B&B retreat is set in a quiet residential zone just outside the city walls. The reception rooms are studded with antiques; the two bedrooms have a shared (but spacious and modern) bathroom. Talia Franceschini is a helpful (English- and French-speaking) hostess. Cash only.

Santo Stefano €–€€ *Via Santo Stefano 84; tel: 051-308 458*; www.bedandbreakfastsantostefano.com. This B&B by the Church of Santo Stefano wins many plaudits for its location and stylish contemporary design. The quietest guest rooms overlook the courtyard, and there are also well-equipped apartments. Weekly rates available.

INDEX

Arca di San Domenico (Tomb of St Dominic) 70

Basilica di San Domenico 69
Basilica di San Petronio 34
Basilica of San Sepolcro 49
Biblioteca Salaborsa 33
Bolognini Chapel 36

Caffè Commercianti 44
Café de la Paix 71
Cappella di San Domenico 69
Casa Isolani 44
Casa Morandi 65
Casa Rossini 44
Cattedrale Metropolitana di San Pietro 61
Chiesa del Crocifisso 49
Collegio di Spagna 71
Collezioni Comunali d'Art 33
Corte Isolani 47
Cortile di Pilato 49

Due Torri 42

Ferrara 79
   Castello Estense 80
   Cathedral 80
   Corso Giovecca 81
   Hostaria Savanarola 80
   Palazzina di Marfisa d'Este 82
   Palazzo dei Diamanti 81
   Palazzo Schifanoia 82
   Piazza della Cattedrale 81
   Pinacoteca Nazionale 81
   Salone dei Mesi 82
Fontana del Nettuno 29

Genus Bononiae project 68

Jewish Ghetto 59

MAMbo 64
Manifattura delle Arti 65
Maranello
   Museo Ferrari 78
markets 94
Martyrium 49
Mercato di Mezzo 40
Modena 76
   Acetaia di Giorgio 76
   Biblioteca Estense 78
   Duomo 77
   Galleria Estense 77
   Museo Enzo Ferrari 78
   Palazzo dei Musei 77
   Palazzo Ducale 78
Museo Civico Archeologico 36
Museo Civico d'Arte Industriale e Galleria Davia Bargellini 46
Museo Civico Medievale 62
Museo della Storia di Bologna 67
Museo delle Cere Anatomiche, L. Cattaneo 56
Museo Ebraico 60
Museo Internazionale e Biblioteca della Musica 45
Museo Morandi 65

Oratorio di Santa Cecilia 52

Palazzo Bevilacqua 71
Palazzo Comunale 32
Palazzo d'Accursio 31
Palazzo Davia Bargellini 46
Palazzo della Mercanzia 44
Palazzo dell'Archiginnasio 38
Palazzo del Podestà 30

Palazzo Fava 61
Palazzo Ghisilardi Fava 62
Palazzo Magnani 50
Palazzo Pepoli Vecchio 67
Palazzo Poggi 54
Palazzo Re Enzo 30
Parma 74
   Baptistery 74
   Camera di San Paolo 75
   Cathedral 74
   Galleria Nazionale 75
   Palazzo della Pilotta 75
   Piazza Duomo 74
   San Giovanni Evangelista 75
   Teatro Farnese 76
Pavarotti, Luciano 78
Piazza della Mercanzia 44
Piazza Galvani 39
Piazza Maggiore 34
Piazza Rossini 51
Piazza San Domenico 69
Piazza Santo Stefano 47
Piazza Verdi 53
Pinacoteca Nazionale 56
Pisano, Niccolò 70
Porta Galliera 64
Porta Magna 35

Ravenna
   Basilica di Sant'Apollinare in Classe 84
   Basilica di Sant'Apollinare Nuovo 84
   Basilica of San Vitale 83
   Mausoleum of Galla Placidia 83
Ravenna 83
Rimini 85
   Tempio Malatestiano 85
Salumeria Simoni 40

San Bartolomeo 43
San Colombano 63
Santuario della Madonna di San Luca 72
San Francesco 66
San Giacomo Maggiore 51
San Martino 60
San Michele in Bosco 72
Santa Maria dei Servi 46
Santa Maria della Vita 41

Santi Vitale e Agricola 49
Santo Stefano 48
Specola 54
Spirito Santo 71
Strada Maggiore 44

Tagliavini Collection 63
Tamburini 40
Teatro Anatomico 38
Teatro Comunale 53

Tombs of the Glossatori 66
Torre degli Asinelli 42
Torre degli Oseletti 46
Torre Garisenda 42

Via Castiglione 67
Via d'Azeglio 71
Via dell'Inferno 59
Via Goito 60
Via Santo Stefano 47

Berlitz® POCKET GUIDE

BOLOGNA

First Edition 2016

Editor: Carine Tracanelli
Author: Susie Boulton
Head of Production: Rebeka Davies
Picture Editor: Tom Smyth
Cartography: Carte
Photography Credits: Alamy 4ML, 7T, 14, 16, 26, 39, 53, 62, 65, 70, 72, 86, 91, 92, 94, 95, 96, 102; Getty Images 4TC, 5MC, 5MC, 6MC, 6TR, 6TL, 7M, 7M, 8L, 17, 18, 20, 22, 25, 28, 32, 41, 47, 51, 56, 60, 75, 84, 98; iStock 5T, 5TC, 5M, 81, 82; Shutterstock 4MC, 4TL, 5M, 6ML, 6ML, 7TC, 8R, 9, 9R, 11, 13, 31, 35, 36, 42, 44, 48, 54, 59, 67, 69, 73, 76, 79; SuperStock 85, 88, 101, 105
Cover Picture: Shutterstock

Distribution
UK, Ireland and Europe: Apa Publications (UK) Ltd; sales@insightguides.com
United States and Canada: Ingram Publisher Services; ips@ingramcontent.com
Australia and New Zealand: Woodslane; info@woodslane.com.au
Southeast Asia: Apa Publications (SN) Pte; singaporeoffice@insightguides.com
Hong Kong, Taiwan and China:
Apa Publications (HK) Ltd; hongkongoffice@insightguides.com
Worldwide: Apa Publications (UK) Ltd; sales@insightguides.com

Special Sales, Content Licensing and CoPublishing
Insight Guides can be purchased in bulk quantities at discounted prices. We can create special editions, personalised jackets and corporate imprints tailored to your needs. sales@insightguides.com; www.insightguides.biz

Contact us
Every effort has been made to provide accurate information in this publication, but changes are inevitable. The publisher cannot be responsible for any resulting loss, inconvenience or injury. We would appreciate it if readers would call our attention to any errors or outdated information. We also welcome your suggestions; please contact us at: berlitz@apaguide.co.uk
www.insightguides.com/berlitz